Open Wide the 4D's

Divorce, Dating, Dentistry & Dildos

Heidi DuBois

If someone had asked me when I was twenty years old to describe my life at forty, never in a million years would I have imagined myself slinging spit as a dental hygienist, selling dildos, Internet dating, and raising my two kids on my own. Yet, this is where I am, and this is my interpretation of the story of my life, "Post-Part Him."

Open Wide
Copyright © 2007 by Heidi DuBois
All rights reserved.
No part of this book may be reproduced without written permission.
Printed in the United States

ISBN-13: 9781517649036
ISBN-10: 151764903X

4th Edition
Edited by Jan Levin
Design and Artwork by Doni Robinson, Vanessa Mendozzi and Natalie DiPaola

Openwide4ds@gmail.com
www.Heididubois.com

This is for my two amazing children, Doni and Jordan. They make each day worth everything. I could not be more proud of the outstanding individuals you both have become.
Nothing is impossible.

Acknowledgements

THIS IS A personal journey, a story about my life immediately following my divorce. Most of these events are factual; I could not have made this stuff up! Some of the events have been moved in time to help the flow of the story and I have altered some of the descriptions and conduct of the people as a courtesy to protect their identities. For the same reasons I have exaggerated and, in some cases, softened some details of certain events.

To my marvelous typical "Jewish mother," Bonnie. Remember, "When you plant potatoes you get potatoes."

I want my entire family to know how much I love them and thank them for always being there and putting up with my craziness.

To Marge, my guru. May your light continue to shine on. You make this world a better place for all you touch.

To all of the many friends I have, some who I have unfortunately lost touch with over the years. The comfort, laughter and times we shared will be cherished forever. I would not have made it without the support.

To the Peters family: thank you for holding me accountable, encouraging me and believing that this was possible, let's complete the vision!

To Neil Stern (Sam): You have been such an important part of this journey, a friend, a confidante and the driving force to get this project completed. Without your many hours of helping me to edit, write and rewrite so many passages in this book, my story would have been much less entertaining and readable than it has turned out.

Lastly, to all of the people who are going through a divorce or breakup, I encourage you to be true to yourself. Take risks, and never stop believing in your dreams. You can do it! Stay tuned for the next book, *Open Wider.*
Heidi

Prologue

IT'S A SATURDAY morning, no different than any other. I'm drinking my coffee and making my kids breakfast when I get a phone call from my friend, Jacqueline. She sounds hysterical. "Heidi, you've got to help me! I need to go to the emergency room!"

Jacqueline and I had been together the night before. She'd attended one of my company's once-or-twice-weekly sex toy parties. I had personally sold her a "Rockin' Robin," a G-spot, clitoral-stimulating vibrator, which billed itself as the Mercedes-Benz of vibrators and sometimes felt like it packed the horsepower of a gasoline-powered lawn mower.

Might her difficulties be related to that purchase? And was this for real, or was she just pulling my leg?

I take another sip of coffee, and butter my kids' toast. I tell her to slow down and to tell me what the problem is. She says the Rockin' Robin had malfunctioned. To be more precise, it had overheated, short-circuited and left her with nasty burns and blisters in some very intimate places. She says she's in terrible pain, and worried about what she's going to say to the doctor.

I've heard a lot of stories about the Rockin' Robin, but I've never heard of one short-circuiting before. Still, such devices are prone to overheating if you leave them on for too long; the instruction manual specifically says not to use it for more than twenty minutes at a time. I'm too discreet to ask exactly what she'd been doing with her Rockin'

Robin to make it overheat, or to ask why she was playing with it on a Saturday morning when the rest of us moms were slugging down lattes and getting our kids off to their hockey games. Instead, I do what any responsible friend and salesperson would; I tell my kids to finish their own breakfasts, I throw a replacement vibrator into my purse, and drive Jacqueline to the hospital.

I can do that with confidence because my close friend and past lover runs the Emergency Department at the nearest hospital here in east suburban Cleveland. I make a call and discover he's on duty this morning. He agrees to treat Jacqueline's injuries — personally — and most importantly, discreetly.

Considering the nature of Jacqueline's wounds and how they were inflicted, I'm expecting a healthy dose of sarcasm and wisecracks from my ex-boyfriend. Instead, I'm impressed at his ability to keep the examination entirely professional. Okay, mostly professional; he's well aware of my line of work, and he can't resist a couple of verbal jabs. But all in all he handles it pretty well, and is even nice enough to step out of the room while a female nurse applies a healing salve to Jacqueline's vagina.

I decide to join him in the hallway to chat. David ("Dr. Dave," as I always call him) looks me over and says, "It's great to see you. Too bad it takes an exploding dildo to get you to visit me." The note of sincerity in his voice tells me this isn't just a "let's get-back-together" line. I blush a bit, though my reverie is interrupted when Jacqueline squeals in pain; the nurse must have hit a particularly tender spot. Dr. Dave checks in on her, then comes back out to reassure me Jacqueline will have a speedy recovery. Then, back to me. "What I'm trying to say, Heidi, is that you look *great*. Are you really as happy and serene as you seem?"

I catch a reflection of myself in a nearby window. I have changed. I'm not the wacky high-energy hurricane I used to be. I begin to think back on the adventures I've had. I'm still a woman in her forties with blonde, curly hair and a curvy body. I still put on scrubs every day to make a living as a dental hygienist to support my children. My face shows a few new laugh lines and a few worry lines, too, yet I'm also still the woman who transformed herself into a sex-toy salesperson and entrepreneur, lecturing on sexual techniques, selling lubes and vibrators to suburban women from 20 to 70 years old. I am a survivor, a proud loving parent of two successful children. I am comfortable in my own skin.

Just as important, I'm convinced there is a lesson in here for women facing challenges, be they marital, financial, emotional, or physical. It's all here in my story. So pour yourself a nice glass of wine, curl up in your favorite chair, and prepare to Open Wide.

1
It all starts with the myth of finding the perfect man and having the perfect life.

I HAD BOUGHT into the fairy tale. Someday I would meet a guy who would be fun, masculine, intelligent, virile, and handsome. He'd have great friends and family and the potential to make enough money to buy a nice house, take us on yearly vacations and put the kids through college without financial aid. He'd be supportive if I wanted to work part-time, and willing to pick up some of the responsibilities with the children.

How naïve could I have been? Very naïve, apparently. The guy on my shopping list was like the supermodels you see on magazine covers; they look great in theory, which is another way of saying they're not real. Once you get past all the airbrushing, Photoshopping and lighting tricks, you discover they actually have pores and warts and pimples and scars and B.O. and may occasionally even fart or take a crap.

One difference between most men and women is that a man fantasizes about how a woman will *look*, while a woman fantasizes about what a man will *do*. That's why men are so easily misled by Photoshop – they WANT to believe that a woman's skin can be completely free from wrinkles or cellulite. But women are guilty of the same misguided thinking, and not just when we look at the cover of *Fitness Magazine* and imagine that such slim hips could ever appear on the same body with such big tits. I did it when I tried to convince myself that every guy I met had potential.

    You'd think I would have learned more from the functionally dysfunctional family I grew up in. In the early 70's my parents, Bonnie and George, were one of the first couples in our entire school district to get divorced. And I was too young to know that the cul-de-sac I grew up on was referred to as the "Swinger Street." My mom quickly became the neighborhood's hottest (and only) divorcee in her Go-Go boots and hot pants. (I never understood why my friends' mothers would keep their husbands away from her till much later on). Meanwhile my father became a swinging bachelor of the seventies; when Steve Martin unveiled his "wild and crazy guy" it was like he was channeling my dad, not the other way around.

    My father, George, who passed away in 2007, was something of an enigma to me. He was a very large, overweight, good-hearted man, much better to other people than he was to his own family. George was a shoe salesman and wannabe entrepreneur. He was always trying to get a bargain, or make a sale. No matter what you would buy, he could get it cheaper, from knock-off purses to refrigerators. His meandering caused him to be in and out of several businesses. Truth is, he was a great salesman, a trait I proudly inherited from him. When it came to his finances, he was a true "live in the moment" kind of guy. Saving or thinking about the future was not a priority for him. At times I felt more like his mother than his daughter.

    My mother, Bonnie, remarried four years after the divorce. Times were different in the 1970's. When Bonnie and Kenny got married, Kenny's two boys, and my brother and I were left completely out of the equation. They got married in Vegas and honeymooned, *sans* kids, in Hawaii. Their friends threw them a big party when they got back home, to which we also weren't invited. We never talked to shrinks about how we felt or how the marriage would change us. A foreign concept today, yet back then it somehow made sense. Maybe because it was all I ever knew. And, maybe, because this was the approach my mom took, I never gave it much thought. It all seemed normal and positive to me.

My mother and stepfather have now been together for more than thirty-five years. Throughout that time we've had a home that has been filled with people and fun, although once you entered into that home your private life no longer existed. As most have come to know, one must be prepared to face Bonnie's rapid-fire questioning. My mother asks questions so fast she doesn't even give you time to answer. She will say, "Can I ask you a question," or " It's not really my business but…". I refer to her as the "human probe," and by the time she's done questioning you, it's like you've had a colonoscopy – maybe not so much fun going through it, but you DO feel better when it's done.

Large family gatherings have always been a part of my life. Parties and holidays for us included exes, in-laws and children from all sides. My family tree is very confusing; we often say you are a true friend if you can expound upon who is related to whom. I grew up thinking all divorced families lived like one big, happy, extended group. Ironically, my family was as abnormal as they come, yet I thought we were normal, and felt proud, not embarrassed, of our normalcy. I could not have imagined my life any other way.

Unfortunately, my children would not have that in their lives.

2
"You have to love and pleasure yourself first."

AS I WALKED down the aisle with my soon-to-be-husband and (eventually) ex-husband, I knew I was making a mistake. I said "I do" even though I knew I shouldn't have, like I do when I throw that chocolate bar in my shopping basket even though I know it will ruin my diet. But it's a familiar story, I'm sure. I was too young and insecure to realize I was supposed to be marrying for love. I was too young to trust my instincts, which told me this guy in a tuxedo was actually a bit of a jerk. And, most fatal of all, I was too young to realize that if a guy isn't being nice to me while we're dating, he sure as hell isn't going to start treating me better when we're married.

Somehow I managed to suffer through more than twelve years of that hell before I got out. I might have gone completely nuts had I not been blessed by the birth of my two kids. They came into the world in the usual painful way, and proceeded to be both a joy and complete pain in the ass to raise, just as they're supposed to be.

And that was exactly what I needed. I could forget how little satisfaction I was getting from my marriage by reveling in my role as the perfect suburban mom. I was PTA volunteer, executive board member, Brownie leader, room mother, party planner, chef, tour guide, psychiatrist, disciplinarian, hand-holder and chauffeur, all rolled into one bosomy blonde package.

To put it another way, I enjoyed everything about being married, except for anything having to do with my marriage. I loved my kids, and my friends. I'd continued working part-time as a dental hygienist. I loved my job, and once I'd concluded that my husband wasn't going to give me the financial security I felt our family needed, I added more days to my work schedule, another great diversion.

It is hard to love a guy if you don't like him. My husband proved it. There were good reasons I didn't like him. I could soft-pedal it and say something like, "We just weren't right for each other," or that "We grew apart" cliché. But that would be a load of crap. The fact is that we started out apart, and then grew even further away from each other.

It is very tempting to spend the rest of this chapter complaining about my ex-husband. In fact, it would be tempting to spend the rest of this book complaining about him, and then turning it into a trilogy in which the next two books complain about him, too. But I'm not going to do that for two reasons. First, it would be a waste of energy and I refuse to focus on the miserable past. Second, I don't want to portray myself as a victim, especially *his* victim; I deserve as much blame as anyone for having put myself in that position in the first place. This story is about redemption, not suffering. It's about getting a new job and moving into a fresh new home – not about how much you hated the last one.

And so, I will leave my ex-husband in the rear-view mirror, looking there occasionally only as a reminder of how far I've come.

But there's a reason the mirror warns us that objects may be closer than they appear; our past is never as far behind us as we'd like to think it is. We continue to be shaped by it even when we'd prefer not to be. And we are at constant risk of repeating our mistakes, no matter how hard we try to avoid them. Sometimes we repeat them precisely *because* we're trying so hard to avoid them. We try so hard to make this next relationship work, that we drive the person away and end up ruining things just like we did the last time. Or, we go too far the other way; insufficient honesty in one relationship leads to excessive honesty in the next one – different causes, but the same result. If you're like me, you really do want to learn from your failures. We always want to do better next time. But, sometimes, we're constrained by who we are. If you keep checking the rear-view mirror you will not see where you're going. But if you never look back, you do so at your peril, too – there just might be a truck barreling down on you, or a really good-looking guy in a BMW convertible, waving at you to pull over so he can get your phone number. You just never know.

3

The Long Winter

FILING FOR DIVORCE was the easy part. Of course, I didn't feel that way that the time. Instead it felt like the hardest thing I'd ever done. My mother said, "When staying is worse than leaving, it is time to get out." I had become the master of making excuses. I was miserable, and everyone – except, perhaps, for me – could see it. I fell asleep unhappy and woke up unhappy. The kids certainly knew it, at least my daughter did. (Boys tend not to notice anything that doesn't involve a ball or a stick). When I finally told my daughter that her father I and were getting divorced she expressed no surprise at all – she looked up from her cereal and simply asked, "Can we stay in this neighborhood?"

As it turned out I'd have preferred she ask me something easy, like "Why don't you and Dad love each other," "What did the ancient rabbis say about divorce," or, "What is the origin of the universe?" But her question about where we would live exposed a serious and embarrassing flaw in my decision-making process – like someone who quits a job without having another one lined up, or knowing whether they qualify for unemployment compensation. I had no idea what to do next.

I knew I would be paying all the bills myself; it seemed a reasonable assumption seeing as how my husband had assured me that this would happen if I went through with the divorce. He also tried to move out when I told him our marriage was over. But he wasn't even reliable in housing decisions; his move out lasted all of three hours.

No, that wasn't a typo. He didn't own much stuff, so moving out consisted mostly of putting his coat on, walking out and driving away. It was lunchtime when he moved out, and it wasn't even dinnertime yet when I heard his car pull back into the driveway. He walked in the front door, which I had foolishly failed to lock, hung his coat back up, and announced, "I've decided I'm not moving out. You can."

This left me two choices. I could wait for him to leave, or, I could leave. Any woman who has ever made the difficult decision to divorce a spouse knows that once you make that decision, you cannot get out fast enough. The thought of spending another hour in the house with this guy, much less weeks or months while he raked me over the coals for having the gall to divorce his ass, made my skin crawl. But Lady Luck – who I think must have been divorced at least once or twice – smiled upon me. My parents happened to be in Florida for the winter, leaving their own home vacant. I didn't even have to ask for a key, since I already had one. So I moved back in with my mom. Not totally, since the kids and the dog stayed behind. I felt a bit like a housekeeper – I would show up in the morning, clean the house, walk the dog, take care of the kids, do everything that needed to be done all day, and then leave to sleep by myself.

It was three miles to get to and from my mother's house. Before long those three miles felt like thirty. As I approached my house each day, I felt like someone who was pushing the plus sides of two magnets together – each day it got a little harder. Finally it was apparent I needed a different approach. Plan A (him moving out) hadn't worked. Plan B (me moving out) hadn't worked out, either. So I decided to move back home and try to identify a Plan C. So, six weeks after I left, I was back. One morning at 5:30, just a week after moving back in, I was on one of my regular morning constitutionals with Gabby (our dog), and my neighbor, Maggie. They were both my confidantes; those days I was willing to talk to just about anyone who would listen. We noticed nothing unusual on the way out; Gabby peed in the usual spots and I regaled Maggie with my usual complaints. On the way back, we turned the corner of our street. It was almost exactly 6 AM, and a man was hammering a For Sale sign into the frozen ground in front of a cute little ranch house. I looked up at Maggie and said, "Is that for real? Do you see that? I'm going to buy that, it's the perfect house for me."

It just felt right. We looked at it that day, and then I brought my parents and children to see it. I made an offer on the house three days later. Although many of my friends criticized me for jumping into it, I knew on every level that I was doing the right thing. Again, I had one of those gut feelings that I was finally starting to pay attention to. Houses like this did not come on the market very often. I scrounged the earnest money from my own savings and hoped to use the proceeds of the sale of our existing house to pay for this one.

I knew I had a long road ahead of me, but at least I'd finally gotten on the entrance ramp.

4

Show Me the Money

DEPENDING ON YOUR point of view, money is the root of all evil, or the lack of money is the root of all evil. Personally, I vote for the lack of money. Or as some comedian once said, "Let me tell you folks, I've been rich, and I've been poor. And it's better to be rich." Neither I nor my ex had ever been rich, but he sure was worried about being poor. At least that's what he used to tell me while trying to make me worry along with him. My impression was that he thought we should stay married because of money. His philosophy seemed to be, so what if we're unhappy, think how much a divorce lawyer would cost! I'd say, "That sounds silly," except that I know there are women out there who are still married today solely because it would be too expensive to get divorced. Some of them have real reason to worry, though others just like the lifestyle they or their kids are living and don't want to give it up. Still others might just be too scared to leave and are using the money to rationalize sticking around. At various times during my marriage I fell into one or more of those categories.

I stayed because I lacked money. I stayed because I feared lacking money. And always I worried about the kids.

Given all that, maybe I should be grateful my ex wasn't rich. It was hard enough saying goodbye to what little we did have; what if I'd also had to give up a boat or a country club membership?

But, for better or worse, I didn't have anything like that to give up. I came out of our divorce with virtually no savings; what little I had I used to set up our new house. And now I also had mortgage payments, utility bills and property taxes to pay, plus all the usual expenses associated with raising two kids in the suburbs – school fees, hockey equipment and baseball uniforms, gasoline to drive them all over creation, doctors' bills and trying to keep up with a few new outfits that fit for all of the Bar/Bat Mitzvahs to which we were invited. Still, I was determined to keep my kids in the same upper-middle class neighborhood. I am not a keep-up-with-the-Jones-type of person, but one way or the other I was determined to make sure my kids wouldn't suffer any more than necessary because of my need to get out of my marriage.

I was making around thirty dollars an hour as a dental hygienist. I ratcheted up from part-time to full-time work as my financial needs escalated. Eventually I was working 5 ½ days a week, on top of all my super-mom activities. But with what seemed to me to be little or no help from my ex, I wasn't making ends meet. I was barely paying for the necessities, much less putting any savings away or being able to afford summer camp and my daughter's Bat Mitzvah. I also hungered for some pampering. Forget yoga classes, a day at the spa, or the shrink I desperately needed; I could barely afford a haircut. Something had to give.

5
Welcome to the Business

SEX COMES IN many ways. For me it arrived in a way that brought both excitement and money. Many books and movies have been based on stories of women who turn to the sex trade for similar reasons. But it happens in real life, too, as it did to me, though in real life the women don't look like Catherine Deneuve or Julia Roberts. In my case I looked like a typical suburban mom, not too bad-looking, and with certain qualities suburban men seem to find attractive, but nobody was going to put me on the cover of Vanity Fair.

Another difference between my life and those fictional stories like *Pretty Woman* or *Belle du Jour* was that the fictional women were selling their bodies. In my case I sold dildos, anal plugs and vibrating cock rings. Does that make me better or worse? Or, was I just another working girl, trying to get by? You tell me.

Here's how I got into the sex industry. I was at a cocktail party, drowning some of my financial worries in a series of martinis. A friend of my family sidled over to me. She had family "connections" – the kind of connections you don't want to write about directly. But the good news was that she was prepared to use those connections to my benefit. She and some other family members had been in the "adult entertainment" business for years. She invited me to work with her. She was vague about what the work entailed, but it had something to do with selling sex toys in peoples' homes in my spare time. Fueled by my financial worries and lubricated by at least three martinis, I said yes.

Later on when I was sober, she explained the details of the deal. Even sober it looked pretty good. Home-toy parties were becoming pretty big business back then. The home parties were nothing new – kitchen conveniences and makeup companies had been doing it for years. What *was* new was the idea of selling sex toys (some people called them "fuckerware parties") in the comfort of one's own home, instead of by mail or in the back of some store in a questionable neighborhood. Trying to capitalize on what they saw as a promising market, several companies started marketing home-toy parties. They were buying the products from my friend's company which, at the time, was one of the largest distributors of sex toys in the Midwest, and then selling them for a substantial profit at home parties. My friend and her family thought that maybe they could run the parties – and capture all the profit – themselves. To do that, all they needed was a product line and someone to work with her to educate and sell to the public.

The company was run by a large family. One of the sisters, who in a bit of kismet was also named Heidi, was put in charge of the home-toy party business. And when she needed someone from the outside to help her, she had come to me. I wouldn't have thought I'd be the obvious choice for something like that; I'd never used a sex toy and I'd only watched a few porn movies up to that point. But the other Heidi was persuasive. She pointed out I was outgoing, blonde, and exuded a "sexual energy." I wasn't sure what that meant but I liked the sound of it. More importantly, I wanted to believe it. She also pointed out that I could use the extra money, which was undeniably true. And the money would be good – she was offering me up to 50% of the gross receipts at any party I worked, depending on the products sold. Looking back on it, I think this outrageously good deal was partly a function of the company's desire to get its foot in the door in this new market. And, it was partly a function of the outrageously big margins they had on most of the products.

But regardless of their reasoning, I was in. The name "Heidi" had to be in there, of course, and so "Heidi's Passion" was born. It was perfect for me – I could truthfully deny that I was "Heidi" if I needed to, but I still got the secret ego boost of working for a company that was, sort of, named after me.

6
Reality Sets In

WHEN YOU ENTER a relationship there is often what I call a "hot water" period of excitement and fantasy, followed by the "cold water" period of reality. You have the giddy period of chase, seduction and exploration, followed by the mundane day-to-day of "okay, we've found each other, but how are we going to make this work in between our day jobs and taking our kids to hockey games and doctors' appointments?"

That was how I felt taking on this new job, or assignment, or project, or business proposal, or whatever I was supposed to call it. The thought of learning about all these new sex toys was very exciting. The thought of making some extra cash was also exciting. And the thought of making a LOT of extra cash was the most exciting of all. But after a week or two, like a good alcohol buzz, the excitement began to fade and the doubts – and headaches – started to creep in.

I had a wide range of doubts. Silly ones like "There is no way I am prepared to talk to a roomful of women about a vibrating plug that goes in their ass." And more serious doubts like how I would feel in "normal" social settings, where everyone in the room knows that I sell sex toys. Would people think that was cool, or would it turn me into a social pariah? Or maybe both?

And then there were the most serious doubts of all – the ones that related to my children. What would it mean to them that their mom had started selling dildos and love swings for a living? I wasn't planning to tell them anytime soon, but they would inevitably find out. Should I tell them before they heard it from someone else? But if so, when would the time be right? And how would they take it?

Initially I was able to put much of that off. When Heidi had first asked me into "the business" I had assumed I would just jump right in and hit the ground running. But the task proved more challenging than I'd expected. Product lines had to created, pricing had to be set, promotional materials needed to be prepared. She developed an ad campaign.

And I soon discovered that she expected me, as the company's #1 salesperson, to sample the products. "See one, do one, teach one." Boxes of samples were delivered to my home; I saw more of the UPS and FedEx men than anyone else for the next few weeks. I did most of my "studying" in my bedroom when my kids weren't home, though occasionally I was able to try something out in the bathroom, usually with the fan on to mask any unintended noise. By the time of our first party I had sampled many of the solo products, but on many others I would just have to wing it. Maybe I could learn a thing or two from my soon-to-be clientele.

You might be wondering what it was like spending all my free time playing with toys specifically designed to give me sexual pleasure. And I will tell you that it sure beat dental floss and mouthwash, by a long shot.

The great majority of these products worked. And I mean, they really, really worked. I was having more orgasms than I'd had in all my prior relationships put together. And I discovered something interesting about myself – the more orgasms I had, the more I wanted! I was horny all the time. At the hockey rink, in the supermarket, walking the dog. I worried whether I was going to turn into one of those laboratory rats in that famous experiment, in which they kept sucking on the cocaine until they died of starvation.

Fortunately I had the ongoing necessities of my six-day-a-week dental hygienist gig, plus all the duties attendant on raising my kids (cooking, cleaning the house, washing clothes, driving them wherever they needed to go) to keep me honest. I was leading a double life and seemed to be getting away with it.

On my bad days I felt more like Heidi Fleiss than Heidi Floss. You remember Heidi Fleiss? She was a high-end suburban Madame, and after her arrest the neighbors were shocked. People thought she was so "nice." Would they say the same about me when my alter ego as the Sex Toy Madame was finally revealed?

I also worried what men would think of all this. Most important, what would the MIWTD's think? (In case you're wondering: Men I Wanted To Date.) Would they be intimidated by a woman who sells sex toys for a living? Would they be put off or assume I was unavailable? Would they assume I was an easy lay, or think I was more interested in sex than in a relationship? Or worse yet, all of the above?

Add to that, my concern that I would become so comfortable with my sex toys that I would stop looking for a man. It seemed possible – after all, these toys were all shaped carefully and ingeniously to do everything a man could do, and more. Plus they never got bored, drank too much, forgot to brush their teeth, or fell asleep before I was done. And if they did, all I had to do was change the batteries and they were ready to go again. There seemed a real risk that I would lock myself in a room with all those toys, and emerge an old woman, doomed to spend her remaining years alone, a sex-toy spinster.

Fortunately (or unfortunately, depending on your point of view), the opposite occurred. All that reading, learning and thinking about sex made me want a man even more, not less. I found that a bit ironic because so many men have told me they worry about women who use sex toys. They worry the toys will be so good that their penises could never compete. But the good news for men is that it doesn't work that way, at least not for most women. Sure, if a guy is lousy in bed, a sex toy will be better, but in that case the problem isn't the vibrator or dildo, it's the guy. Human touch is irreplaceable – you can't kiss or spoon with a dildo. Orgasms weren't enough, I wanted emotion and intimacy. It was the difference between getting laid, and making love.

To put it another way: the more satisfied I felt sexually, the less satisfied I felt emotionally. It all seemed so unfair.

7

Signs, Signs, Everywhere Signs

IF YOU'VE EVER tried thinking two contrary thoughts at the same time, you know it doesn't work very well. It's called cognitive dissonance. It comes from being presented with two contrary sets of facts and trying to believe both of them. In my case it was worse. I had at least three contrary sets of facts to try to embrace. In one world I was the highly competent professional dental hygienist, chatting up my patients, happy, confident, good at what I do, earning a decent living. In another world I was the supermom, successfully parenting my kids, getting them to school, doctors' appointments and practices on time, helping them with their homework, doing their laundry, and giving them advice whether they wanted it or not. In another world I was living in a house with a man I didn't love and who, by all appearances, hated me and used every opportunity he had to put me down, tell me how worthless I was, and that I couldn't survive without him.

And yet now, I had another world, in which I was a free-wheeling, risk-taking entrepreneur preparing to walk into peoples' homes selling sex toys, playing with them myself and my exploding libido in the meantime. And, finally, I had a world in which I was just plain lonely – I had a wealth of friends, professional colleagues, neighbors and family members, but nobody could bridge the gap for me between all the different worlds I was trying to live in. It was just too much for my fragile brain, and one day it just all seemed to converge at one time.

When I finally snapped it was because of a pimple. Well, it was more like a cyst. I'd been invited to a Bat Mitzvah party which was going to be a particularly large, lavish and well-attended affair, and I secretly harbored hopes of meeting an eligible and hopefully horny, open-minded and financially stable (in that order) divorced man. I bought a new dress that I couldn't afford. I had everything lined up. In my own mind I was already meeting the perfect man, getting wined, dined and laid, all thanks to that party.

But I then learned how Cinderella must have felt when her bitchy step-sisters told her she couldn't go to the ball. Less than forty-eight hours before the party, I saw the dermatologist about an annoying bump on my forehead that wouldn't go away. She took one look and told me it needed to be removed. She said it would be a "minor" procedure, though I had long since figured out that the only truly "minor" procedure is one that is performed on someone else. And this was no exception. The doctor misjudged or misdiagnosed my cyst, and the quick little procedure she'd promised me turned into a two-hour marathon of digging and scraping. It took me yelling "get the fuck out of my head" for her to realize she couldn't get the whole thing out in her office.

I woke up the next morning with one side of my face covered with black-and-blue bruises; it looked like I'd just fought for the welterweight boxing championship and gotten the stuffing beaten out of me. Desperate for social interaction, I stupidly decided to go to the Bat Mitzvah party anyway. I went to the salon and had my hair done up to cover as much of my face as possible, and I bought purple eye shadow straight from the 80's in an attempt to make my good eye look as purple as my bad one. I swallowed one of the Vicodins the dermatologist had mercifully given me, and headed out the door. After all, this was the night I was going to meet "him" and nothing was going to stop me.

The evening turned out to be everything I'd been hoping for, and much less. There were lots of eligible guys there, but I didn't get to know any of them because once I turned around and they saw my purple face and swollen eye, they would mumble something about needing another drink or seeing a friend across the room, and vanish. At one point I went to the bathroom, looked in the mirror and even terrified myself; it seemed that the hairdo and makeup had made things worse, not better. Instead of looking like Cinderella I looked like a hooker trapped in the 1980s. Distracted by my horror, I headed straight to the bar and downed a martini, completely forgetting the Vicodin I'd taken earlier. Next thing I knew I was deathly sick and had to be driven home.

Or so I was told the next day, seeing as how I couldn't remember anything that happened after I swallowed that martini. The whole thing left me feeling physically and emotionally desolate. There wasn't a molecule in my body that didn't feel miserable, and there wasn't a thought in my head that didn't involve some kind of misery. By Monday morning I had thought I'd pulled myself together a bit, but apparently I was wrong. When I walked into work that morning, my boss, the dentist, took one look at me, made a face and said, "You look like shit. Take my advice, you need to run away from home for a while." I think he was partly worried about my emotional state and partly worried that I would scare his patients away. And in either case I decided he was right. So I made three phone calls. The first was to *Continental Airlines* to buy a plane ticket to Boca Raton, where my parents were staying for the winter. The second was to my parents, to tell them I was coming and to pick me up at the airport.

The third was to my soon-to-be-ex-husband. I told him that for the coming weekend he was completely responsible for the kids. He said, "What do you mean? What am I going to do with them?" Our kids were twelve and eight, so I figured it was time for him to learn. "I don't care, I'm sure you'll think of something," was all I said.

I had a few patients to see that day, but as soon as I was done scraping their plaque and polishing their molars, I cut out of the office, went home, packed my stuff and took off for the airport. I didn't bring much – a couple of changes of clothes, a bikini, my journal, and some meditation tapes. I left the toys behind because I was afraid of airport security finding them and deeming me a threat to society, but I didn't want to entirely waste my time either, so I brought the entire pile of sex books I'd picked up for my Heidi's Passion research. I thought it would make for some good beach reading.

My parents met me at the airport and expressed the appropriate concern about my well-being. I had to reassure them that my bruises had been inflicted by my dermatologist and not by my husband. I also tried to reassure them I was okay emotionally, although I certainly didn't believe it myself. I felt like writing a sequel to that 1970s self-help book, *"I'm OK, You're OK,"* except my book was going to be entitled, "Neither Of Us Is OK, So Let's Just Stop Pretending." I fell into bed exhausted, looking forward to a day on the beach, alone with my tapes and books.

The next day I stuffed myself into my bikini, walked to the beach and found a spot as far from anyone else as I could manage. I got my crying out of the way early, and then decided to try some meditation before moving on to the sex books. So I put in a Chakra meditation tape and closed my eyes. I did what it told me. I tried to clear my head by feeling the earth, listening to the ocean, and enjoying the smells. I wanted to connect with the Universe, find my Center, do all the things that the yogis tell you will make the difference between the serene, supremely content people they were and the miserable excuse for a woman I felt I was. I asked the universe to show me a sign letting me know whether I was on the correct path. I had so many questions for the Universe: "Will I be okay?" "What about my kids?" "Will I find true love someday?" "Am I destined to be alone?" "Will I ever find a man who has even heard of the G-spot, much less be able to find it?"

I felt myself drift away, lost in my meditations. I waited for the sign, not really expecting one but hoping anyway. I was drifting happily in my solitude when I heard some strange noises working their way past my headphones. It sounded as if I had been transported into the middle of some kind of party. I opened my eyes and saw a group of people standing next to my blanket and others running toward it. There were maybe a couple of dozen of them in all. And they weren't just ordinary people. They were all young guys, suntanned, muscular, in matching orange, skimpy Speedo bathing suits. It was hard to imagine this was really happening. In fact I was convinced it wasn't really happening so I closed my eyes and reopened them. My meditation tape was still running, telling me to cleanse my mind, but how was I supposed to do that with these guys in their Speedos surrounding my blanket? Why were they were here? Yes, I'd asked the Universe for a sign, but was group sex with a bunch of twenty-year-old Florida lifeguards really what the Universe had in mind for me?

Not that there necessarily would be anything wrong with that...

I will confess that my first thought was not curiosity over who these guys were or why they were there. Rather my first thought was to hope one would lean over and start rubbing oil on my body. But that didn't happen. Instead they just stood there, looking at me. Then a couple of them noticed my reading materials: books like *"Tickle His Pickle"* and *"How to Achieve Multiple Orgasms in Three Easy Steps."* I heard some chuckles and suddenly felt grateful that the book *"Anal Pleasures"* was at the bottom of the stack.

My tape intoned vociferously, almost at a yell, "Open your heart Chakra, open and let love in!" Okay, enough was enough. I sat up, hit the stop button on the tape player, and said, "What is going on? Who are you guys?"

One of them responded, "Lady, you're in the middle of lifeguard training." I wasn't sure I liked being called "Lady." It made me feel old, even though it was true I was probably much closer in age to his mother than I was to him. But somehow I felt my mojo coming back. I threw my arms out, splayed out on the blanket, and yelled, "Quick, I need CPR, somebody help me!" I half-expected one of them to go with it, jump on me and give me rapid chest compressions and a deep lip lock. But nothing happened. I looked up again and they were all staring at me, as if trying to figure out whether I was serious. Or, for all I knew, maybe I'd just violated some city ordinance prohibiting false lifeguard calls, and they were going to write me a ticket?

Then the Speedo boys started laughing. One of them asked me if I was some kind of sex therapist. I explained my new business and why I was doing all that reading. I was pretty excited to be having this conversation, and I remember very little about their faces. I laughed and joked and flirted with them. I hinted at some discomfort some of them might have been feeling in their Speedos. They went along with it and offered to save me from my "distress." Eventually they offered, rather apologetically, that they needed to return to their training. And the best part was, it turned out that I was fine where I was.

And so I had my Sign from the Universe. The sign said, "Well-built lifeguards in skimpy Speedos will appear if you want them to." And that was good enough for me.

8
Time to Party

MEMORIES OF GLISTENING, six-pack abs still fresh in my mind, I returned home with a new sense of purpose and a burst of energy, as if I'd just finished a five-gallon time-release Frappuccino. The court date for my divorce was finally set for late spring. The house was on the market, and a new home was beckoning. Life was looking up!

Of course none of that changed the fact that I still needed money — more so than ever, now that I was facing paying for a house on my own. I'd been "studying" my collection of sex toys and manuals for a while now. It was time to actually have a party. Our website was close to completion, along with a printed catalog. My presentation was coming together nicely, but I needed to practice in front of a live audience.

I felt I might be more comfortable in front of an audience I knew, so I asked some of the girls at work whether I could try out my presentation on them. They all knew about my new line of work anyway since I had a tendency to talk incessantly about it at work. They made comments that had led me to believe they might be interested, and it turned out I was right. In fact, they proved to be more than just interested; when I raised the idea, they responded enthusiastically as if to say, "It's about time you asked us!"

Amy volunteered to have the party in her basement. I worked with six women. I encouraged them to invite friends, and most of them did. We ended up with about two dozen people in Amy's basement, ranging from twenty-three to fifty-three years old. I felt naughty and excited at the same time, which I came to discover was how most of my customers were feeling, too.

Our marketing pitch was pretty slick. We had little Heidi's Passion's goodie bags to give away at the end, with or without a purchase. Each bag had coupons to the all-male revue we were sponsoring at a local dance club every Friday night, a Heidi's Passion pen, a coupon giving you 20% off your purchase if you booked a party, small flavored lubricant samples, and our best-selling, can't-live-without "Magic Bullet." The Bullet was a small, egg-shaped battery-operated device which vibrated at multiple speeds. It can be used on various parts of the body, inside or outside, and it works on both a male or female. I had discovered the joys of the Bullet early in my own product trials, and I didn't need to fake my enthusiasm for it in my presentations.

We had also come up with the idea of what we called "Passion Dollars." It was like a kickback (though we preferred the term "incentive") to anyone who hosted a party. The hostess would receive not just a "hostess gift" but also a credit toward free products, based on a percentage of what her guests spent. This meant the hostess had a strong motive not just to host the party in the first place, but also to bring in as many guests as she could and, most importantly, to encourage them to spend their money.

The night of my first party, I packed up my lipstick-red PT Cruiser (yes, I drove a PT Cruiser, a constant reminder not to let your mother go car-shopping with you) with about a hundred sample items and plenty of stock. I drove well under the speed limit and came to a complete stop at every stop sign, out of fear I'd have to explain my carful of dildos to the police. At my suggestion Amy told her husband he had to leave the house and that he couldn't return until the party was over. Amy and her husband were in their mid-twenties, which led to my first lesson in generational responses to my parties. In older couples (early forties and up), the men wanted nothing to do with these parties. They were more than happy to give their women cash and credit cards and get out of Dodge to ponder the purchases that would await them on their return.

But the younger guys, like Amy's husband, were different. I pulled into the driveway in my dildo-filled car, and started unloading my products just as Amy's husband and his buddies were heading out. They showed great interest in the boxes I was carrying into the house, and went out of their way to help me carry them in, probably because so many of the product packages had photos of sexy women and couples in suggestive poses. Which makes sense, of course. If you want to sell applesauce, put a photo of some ripe juicy apples on the label. If you want to sell a male masturbation sleeve, put a photo of some ripe, juicy breasts on the label. Or if it's an edible lube, put a photo of a woman and a guy, with the woman.... Anyway, you get the idea. "Truth in advertising," I call it.

Heidi had driven to the party separately because she had a bunch of stuff to carry herself. Once all the products were downstairs it took us nearly an hour to set everything up, put batteries in all of the demo products and organize the merchandise. Heidi concentrated on the paperwork and sales materials, while I focused on making the products appear as user-friendly as possible. We divided the basement into two areas. One was an open area where everyone would gather for the party and for product demos. The other was a private area for purchases and questions.

The private area was a crucial part of the sales process. Although some women were completely comfortable asking questions and conducting their business in public, most preferred to keep their personal preferences, questions, and concerns out of the public eye. If a woman's husband or boyfriend liked to have a finger in his ass during sex – or if she did – she didn't feel a need to share that fact with the rest of the neighborhood. The private area gave her the freedom to confide in us and explore products for her particular "needs," without having to worry that the next morning the moms at the playground would be talking about her vibrating nipple clamps. So our private area became a cross between a gynecologist's office and a psychiatrist's couch – no holds barred, and total discretion guaranteed.

Finally everything was set up and the party began. Heidi and I introduced ourselves and Heidi's Passion. We explained how the evening would work, and gave our sales pitch on how to book future parties. Because this was my first party, I'd prepared note cards on each product. I went through each one that we'd brought samples of, three or four dozen in all. I explained how to use it, when to use it, who to use it on, where to put it, and what it feels like. We passed lubes and massage oils for tasting, smelling and feeling. We tried to engage all of their senses. Well, almost all – that last one would have to wait for their bedrooms!

To my surprise, one of my co-workers invited a couple of her friends who were also my professors from dental school. I was accustomed to seeing these women in the front of a room demonstrating items like dental X-Ray holders and tooth scalers. They were cool, trained professionals. And here I was in the front of the room, explaining to them the functions and effects of a clitoral-stimulating vibrator. It might have seemed a bit absurd, were it not for the excitement in the room. I couldn't believe it – these women were seriously horny!

True, there was some initial nervousness in the room. I know I was nervous at first. I was nervous about how all these women would react to an in-your-face discussion of sex toys. And I felt they were a bit nervous, too, though I suppose I may have just been projecting my own anxieties onto them. In any event, after about ten or fifteen minutes any nervousness I felt or sensed was completely gone. By the time I got around to giving the attendees blowjob instructions, I might as well have been explaining how to use a toothbrush. I gave them a sample of "Good-Head," which numbs the mouth so the gag reflex won't interfere with fellatio. Not too different from the topical anesthetic we used in the office for dental procedures.

I guess I shouldn't have been surprised that a roomful of dental people would be into oral sex. But it wasn't until I started talking about vibrators that things really started getting interesting.

9

On With the Show

LIKE I SAID, the young guys like Amy's husband were different. And he proved it when he decided to crash the party. He brought six of his friends, too. They were 25 years old, and ranged from decent-looking to never-in-a-million-years. They were also drunk.

So here was the scene. We had a basement full of women who had spent the past hour talking about sex and playing with sex toys. Then six intoxicated and horny twenty-five-year-old guys wandered in. I didn't feel comfortable asking them to leave – this was Amy's basement, not mine, and she seemed fine with them being there. In fact, I was surprised to discover that pretty much everyone seemed fine with it. And the customer is always right. So while the guys joked around in the back, I continued my presentation.

For better or worse the boys had happened in at the beginning of my discussion of female G-spot orgasms. I went on, explaining that the thing about the G-spot is that it can be challenging to find. But if you have the right partner, the right position, and/or the right toys, the sky is the limit. I started to describe how they could help their partners help them find it and how they could try to find it on their own. I also demonstrated which of the various dildos and vibrators we were selling would make that process a little easier.

What I hadn't anticipated while preparing my presentation, was that there would be men in the room. And not just any men, but drunk young guys near the peak of their virility. The boys seemed unimpressed when I showed an anatomical representation of the uterus, and tried to describe clinically the location of the G-spot a few inches up the vaginal wall, on the anterior or front side. They perked up, though, when I started explaining how a woman's partner can reach it (easiest way is with the female sitting up, straddling and facing her partner), and by the time I got to explaining the G-spot orgasm itself, including female ejaculation, they seemed to be eying the room, trying to decide which women might be candidates for trying this stuff out with them.

To me this represented a welcome change in attitude. There is a joke I've heard men tell, which says more about the male psyche than I think most men would want to admit. It goes like this:

> Q: How do you give a woman an orgasm?
> A: Who cares?

Sadly, I think more than just a few women have bought into that, too. Early on we're told (mostly by men) that our own pleasure is less important than a man's pleasure. If the guy doesn't cum that's a disaster, we must be doing something wrong. But if *we* don't orgasm, that's okay. And worse case, we can always fake an orgasm. Why would any woman want to do that? I was there to tell my female customers that their pleasure mattered, too. In fact there was an entire industry out there, devoted largely to developing products specifically for giving them that pleasure. And if they chose to buy some of those products from me, so much the better. I was getting 50%, plus the use of demos at home. Cash and orgasms. Who could ask for a better combination?

Well, maybe cash, orgasms, and a relationship with that horny, liberal and financially stable guy I was looking for. But it seemed that was going to have wait for a while.

So, for the time being, things were looking up. Despite the invasion by Amy's husband and his posse, or maybe because of it, we had great sales numbers – we grossed about eight hundred dollars that night. The biggest sellers were small personal vibrators, plus various couples' enhancements like lubes, massage oils, and silk scarves (they're great for tying your partner's hands or wrists to the bedposts, and they can double as a blindfold). I walked out of the party with $400 cash in my purse, excited at the prospect of paying off the gas bill and the electric bill in the same month.

That night, I had discovered what I called the Multiple C-Note Orgasm. It's the orgasm you experience when you have a stack of hundred-dollar bills in your dresser drawer. Not quite a G-spot orgasm, but it would certainly do for now.

10
Ready to Date

SO THERE I was, working six days a week digging in people's mouths, and in the evenings, hawking sex toys to horny housewives. For the first time since the split I was not just barely making ends meet, but was actually paying bills and putting some money into savings. I could imagine being able to afford a Bat Mitzvah party somewhere other than Dunkin' Donuts. The only thing I didn't have was a social life. I don't mean not enough of a social life, or an unsatisfying social life. I mean, NO social life. What passed for my social life consisted of an occasional thirteen year-old's Bat or Bar Mitzvah and a morning dog-walk with my next-door-neighbor. I started to feel an itch to start dating, like a mosquito bite that just wouldn't go away. I was offered a series of fix-ups, but they were almost entirely from my mother's friends, which made me suspicious. When I'd let her help me choose a car I ended up in a PT Cruiser that made me look like a character from a not-very-funny sit-com; I shuddered to think what would happen if I allowed her to be involved in choosing my next boyfriend, which seemed to leave me just one option: Internet dating.

I might have expected my mother to be all for it, as her anxiety over my not having a husband was consuming her. Before long she began mentioning it almost daily, until I decided I'd better put up a profile before she did it for me.

I had heard all the horror stories about people lying on dating sites. Lies that ranged from "fudging" the truth, like saying you're

31 years old when you're really 41, to gross misrepresentations, like saying you're a tenured university professor when you're actually an unemployed dishwasher, or claiming to be single when you're actually married with 5 kids under the age of 8. I decided to avoid not just the big lies, but the small ones, too. I was honest about everything. I admitted that the judge had not yet signed off on my divorce. I mentioned that I had two kids living in my house. I confessed that I had mixed feelings about starting to date and that I was worried whether I really had enough time to do it.

I also made sure the men would know what I really looked like. I had heard, and would soon discover for myself, that many men and women on dating sites posted misleading photos of themselves, photos that showed what they looked like many years or many pounds ago. I posted a recent photo that showed me in full bloom – my hair, breasts and inches were there for everyone to see. After all, if nobody expressed any interest, then I wouldn't have to risk going out on dates or getting involved or hurt. I could tell my mom I had tried, and go back to my life of dental scrubs and dildo sales.

Oh, yes, the dildos. I almost forgot about those. I said earlier that I was honest about "everything." I decided that discretion trumped honesty when it came to the sex toy business. I didn't have much (read, "any") experience with Internet dating, but I didn't need experience to know it would be a bad idea to put into my profile any mention of dildos, floggers, anal beads, cock rings, or G-spot orgasms. I may have been naïve, but I wasn't stupid.

And so my true-as-far-as-it-went profile went live. I posted it, turned off the computer and went to work. I hoped I'd get a couple of hits, and maybe a date, or two. Silly me.

11

The Dating Game

IN THE FIRST twenty-four hours my profile was up, more than 200 people had viewed it; after 48 hours that number was up over 300. (I hoped they were all men, though I had no way to tell). Out of those hundreds of viewers I got about 75 messages. I had no idea whether that was a good percentage, though I assumed it was, and at first I was excited to have all those emails to go through. Every time I opened one I wondered whether this guy might be "the one."

My optimism started to fade pretty quickly, though. The first thing I noticed was that not many of the messages were from guys who lived anywhere near me. The profile form didn't ask, "Do you want a pen pal?" (The answer would have been "no"), or, "Are you interested in a long-distance relationship?" (Also, no). But it did ask, "Would you be willing to relocate for the right relationship?" My answer was no. But that didn't seem to slow down a bunch of men from all over the world. In those first couple of days alone I got messages from Israel, Sweden, Russia, Canada and South Africa. The messages said things like, "Hi, I saw your profile I think you're beautiful," or, "Hi, I live half way around the world but I just wanted to say hi." Or, "Hi, you have a nice smile." And one began, "Hi, I know we'll never meet, but...".

What were these guys thinking? What were they looking for? Were they so lonely or horny that they were willing to spend their time writing to women all over the world in the hope of getting a bite?

Were they hoping for phone sex, or the email equivalent of phone sex? (Sexting wasn't around yet.) Or were they looking for something else? At the time I couldn't imagine what that "something else" might be, so I just deleted every message from anyone who would have required a plane ticket and/or a passport to meet.

Just like that, 70% of my potential dates disappeared.

And the rest soon disappeared for other reasons. For instance, in addition to the geographically-ridiculous messages, there were the graphically-ridiculous messages. One man had a photo that showed him playing the guitar half-naked. The message asked, "Will you strum my string?" And as bad as his sense of humor (and lack of modesty) was, his body was worse. He was overweight, with manboobs prominently displayed. If he'd been buff I could have imagined him getting some responses – maybe even from me – but when I saw his picture, all I could think, was "yuck." And no matter how long it had been since I'd been out on a date, I still knew that "yuck" was not a good way to start a relationship.

Another guy had posted a photo in which he was surrounded by various wildlife, including lizards, snakes, and birds. At first I thought he might be a veterinarian but his profile said he was an accountant. Maybe he was an animal rights supporter or had a zoo for a client, who knows? But in the forefront of the photo was a cat. The guy's message referred to the photo, and said, "Take a look at my profile photo, the only thing I care about is the pussy."

I tried to convince myself the guy was demonstrating a great sense of humor. But instead I decided that only a loser would introduce himself that way. I couldn't help wondering how many women he'd tried that line on. I wanted to know whether it had ever worked – and if it had, I wanted to meet the woman it had worked on, and tell her how sorry I felt for her.

And so on. As I continued to hit "delete" I began to feel some self-doubt. Was I being too harsh? Was I expecting too much? Maybe these crass, blatantly sexual overtures were the norm these days? After all, I'd been out of the dating world for fifteen years, maybe things had changed? I showed some of my messages to the girls at work.

The first one I showed them was the guy with animals who "only cared about the pussy." My co-workers promptly named him "Pussy Boy." They had a great time constructing a back story for him, how various unfortunate childhood traumas had led to his fixation on pussies, and what that would mean for our relationship. Whether he preferred to be on top or bottom (we decided bottom) and whether that was good or bad (they thought it was good, I wasn't so sure). They were having so much fun speculating about him that they wanted me to go out with him, just to see what the real story was. It was easy for them, of course, since it was my pussy on the line, not theirs. So I resisted their pressure. But little did I know that my mom would soon be urging me to go out with him, too. And if you can't trust your own mother to defend the sanctity of your pussy, who can you trust? You are no doubt wondering, how or why my mother would have come to even know about Pussy Boy, much less to encourage me to date him. First of all you have to understand that my mother and I had a relationship that was as much girlfriend-girlfriend as it was mother-daughter. I've always told her pretty much everything. So it felt normal for me to show her the various messages I was getting on-line, and to tell her about Pussy Boy. I also showed her the photos.

A couple of weeks later I was in my kitchen enjoying a rare moment of peace and quiet when the phone rang. My mother had been volunteering at a local hospital. She called me directly from the hospital, probably risking setting off some guy's pacemaker with her cell phone, to let me know she'd just met Pussy Boy's mother, who was in for surgery. I asked the obvious question – how could she have possibly figured out that she'd met Pussy Boy's mother?

She replied, "Pussy Boy is here visiting her. And he's pretty cute. You should come meet him."

Great. Most Jewish mothers want their daughters to meet, date, marry and procreate with a nice Jewish boy. My mother wanted me to do it with a guy who freely admitted before he'd even met me, that his number one concern was pussies? I said, "Mom, listen to yourself. Are you really trying to fix me up with a guy that even you call 'Pussy Boy'?" I wasn't mad at her, but I didn't mind letting her wonder whether I was or not. (Jewish guilt can be wonderfully motivating when used properly). I told her to feel free to try to fix Pussy Boy up with any of the nurses there, or even one of her friends' daughters, but to leave my pussy out of it. I hung up and went back to my cappuccino. For better or worse, my pussy was going to remain off-limits to men for at least a little while longer.

12
Fixed up and Stuck up

THE NEXT DAY my mom called me at work. She said she'd chatted a bit with Pussy Boy and discovered he was "a little weird." I was tempted to ask what she meant, since apparently she didn't think it was "a little weird" to introduce himself with a statement referring to his love for pussy. But I decided I preferred not to know. Instead I thanked her and asked her to try to remember this experience the next time she wanted to fix me up with her best friend's next-door-neighbor's accountant's brother-in-law's cousin. And I told her I had to get back to work, which was true.

From my point of view it's very easy to carry on a conversation with a patient at a dentist's office. I can talk whenever I want, and my patients can only talk when I let them. On this particular morning I decided to let the patient do some extra talking because she was trying to fix me up with her accountant. The first thing I did, of course, was to make sure it wasn't Pussy Boy. I was relieved that it wasn't, as she described someone tall with dark hair, neither of which was true for Pussy Boy. In fact, her accountant sounded like your basic Nice Guy, which, in retrospect, should have immediately made me suspicious. Anyway, when I agreed to meet him, she asked for my cell phone number, which I gave her. She said she would tell him to call me, and then winked at me and said, "Don't worry, all I'll tell him is that you're a hygienist." I was taken aback for a moment, trying to figure out what she meant by that. And then I remembered that she'd been at one of my parties the previous week. Amazingly, I still hadn't figured out what I'd say to guys I was dating about my "second job," or how early on I would tell them. All I knew was that I needed to keep it to myself as long as I could – if the girls at the office named that last guy "Pussy Boy," I could only imagine what a future boyfriend's pals might nickname me. Dildo Heidi?

The Nice Guy accountant called me. We met for coffee. He was pretty normal, which unfortunately is another way of saying he was boring. He was neither good-looking nor not good-looking. There was nothing particularly right or wrong about his personality. His jokes weren't bad, but they weren't quite good, either. After what I'd been through in my marriage I guess I should have found "not bad" to be pretty attractive, but I was looking for more. Plus, in my effort to make conversation, I made the mistake of telling him about Pussy Boy and mentioning he was also an accountant. His response was, "Oh, he must be Jewish." I had no idea what he meant by that, and decided I didn't really care. I thanked him for the coffee, and pretended that I needed to get home. He said he'd call me, and I tried to act as indifferently as I could, though for all I knew, maybe boring accountants were turned on by indifference. I was, after all, new at this.

So now I had three kinds of men on my no-date list: guys who mention pussy in their on-line profiles; patients' accountants; and anyone my mother liked. Who was next?

Apparently it was Orthodox Jews. I had continued to receive messages from guys responding to my Internet dating profile and had responded to a few. There was this one guy who was, for a change, appropriately friendly without being inappropriately forward. He said he was a businessman, though he didn't specify what kind of business, and I was so grateful he'd sent me three messages without mentioning sex, that I didn't ask any questions, except to ask "Where?" when he said he'd like to meet. We agreed to meet for drinks at 4 P.M. one Wednesday, which for me was right after work. I explained to him I was coming from work and that I would be in scrubs. (Not to worry, I change into clean ones before I leave work each day, so I'll have them for the next day and I don't have to carry the dirty ones back and forth). He said that was great, and that he was looking forward to meeting me.

We met at my favorite neighborhood bar. It was hard not to notice right away that he was wearing a black suit on a pretty hot day, and had the signature white strings – Tzitzit – hanging below his jacket. He was an Orthodox Jew. It seemed strange to me that he hadn't mentioned that in his messages or on his profile. He reassured me it didn't bother him that I wasn't observant. (Actually, for me, "observance" meant watching Seinfeld reruns and eating an occasional bagel for breakfast). But all in all he seemed friendly and harmless enough. We talked about all the things you would expect to talk about on a first date – dating war stories, food preferences, friends, family histories. We spent about an hour together and at the end he invited me for dinner the following Saturday, after sundown, of course. He did not mention the scrubs I was wearing and after a while I forgot I was wearing them.

The guy wasn't striking me as Mr. Right, or even Mr. Almost Right. But my mother always said, "You never know who you'll meet through someone else." I know that sounds a bit mercenary – going out on a date with someone because you hope he might introduce you to someone else. But people have gone out on dates for much worse reasons. So I said yes.

I run into my dental hygiene patients all the time all over the place – at the mall, the grocery store, hockey games, to name just a few. And it's not uncommon for my patients to tell me, in one way or another, "Heidi, I hardly recognize you in clothes." I wish I could say that is a comment on the exciting, sex-filled life I'd been leading. But it was instead a comment on how hard it is to see the shape of my body through a set of scrubs. Some male doctors I know like to wear scrubs in public because it says to women, "Look at me, I'm a doctor." (Male nurses sometimes wear them too, hoping women will mistake them for doctors). But on a woman, scrubs say "Don't mind me, I just came from work."

After our date I had gone home, cleaned the kitchen a bit, gotten out of my scrubs and into some pajamas, and checked my emails. I saw one from my new Orthodox friend. Even though I wasn't that excited about him, I was still happy to see that he was pursuing me. I assumed his email would contain flattering comments about how much he enjoyed meeting me and how much he was looking forward to seeing me again. Wrong. It said, "Thank for you for meeting me tonight, looking forward to Saturday. Please send a photo of yourself in a bathing suit. Your scrubs were not very revealing."

Really? At first I thought it must be a joke, but he hadn't impressed me as having much of a sense of humor, plus his email showed no sign of joking. So I responded, "Thank you for meeting me tonight, too. And I want to thank you. I was so impressed with your religiosity that I have decided to become Orthodox, myself. Of course, this means that I cannot appear in public with bare shoulders or legs, or without a wig. So I cannot send you the photo you requested. Also, I just remembered I have to go to the Mikvah [an Orthodox Jewish ritual bath] to wash my hair Saturday night, so I can't go out with you. But in the meantime I'd suggest calling your rabbi. Maybe he will have photos of some female congregants in bathing suits hidden in his office. So thanks, good luck, and don't forget to think of me while you're praying."

Actually I didn't write any of that, though I wish I had. Instead I just wrote, "You are nuts. And you should look elsewhere for a date next Saturday night. Goodbye."

Meanwhile the emails kept coming. I started exchanging emails with another guy, a forty-something man from a couple of suburbs over. We'll call him Bill. Bill mentioned that he had formed a support group for newly divorced people to meet and hang out. He said it wasn't a dating service, rather he was trying to create a no-pressure environment where people who wanted someone to talk to could just get together as friends. This sounded very attractive to me. In fact, it sounded better than a date, especially after the kinds of dates I'd been having. I asked if I could come to the next get-together and bring a girlfriend.

Bill said he'd prefer that I come alone. Supposedly this was to see if I would be a "good fit" with the rest of the group. This should have been a giant red flag, even as naïve as I was. But I was so excited to be getting out to meet people that I decided to go anyway. I also felt pretty safe, since the meeting was going to be at a local wine bar that I'd been to many times. Plus, the bartender was a patient of mine. So I showed up. And I ignored his request to come alone – I took my sex-toy-party business partner Heidi with me, because she also happened to be going through a divorce at the time. We both figured that nothing could possibly happen at this restaurant that would be as intimidating as standing up in front of a group of thirty women with a vibrator in one hand and a cock ring in the other. So we did ourselves up, got to the restaurant a few minutes early, and grabbed a couple of seats at the bar.

I started chatting up the guy next to me, who turned out to be very good-looking, very friendly, and very married. I told him why I was there, and we had some fun trying to guess who else at the bar might be a support group member. After a few minutes of our guessing game, Bill arrived. He looked pretty much the same as his picture, which I considered a good sign. (If a guy shows you a misleading photo, what else is he going to mislead you about?) Though ironically, it was Bill who was soon accusing me of misleading him! I greeted him warmly and introduced him to Heidi.

Bill and Heidi began chatting as my conversation with Mr. Married Guy was winding down. Then I felt a tap on my shoulder. It was Bill. He leaned over to whisper in my ear. I was expecting something cute, or some interesting secret about some of the people I was going to meet tonight. Or maybe even a come-on. Instead his voice turned into a hiss, like I was suddenly talking to a rattlesnake. He said, "You are the rudest, most stuck-up person I've ever met. I told you to come alone. I thought you and I were going to hook-up but obviously you had no intention of going on a date with me. You're here under false pretenses."

Huh? I couldn't believe my ears. This guy thought we were going to "hook up?" What planet was he living on? Was he psychotic? Or a serial killer who was upset that he couldn't get me alone? Regardless of the truth, I was waffling between astonishment and anger. I took a deep breath, and stared him down, which wasn't so hard since I was at least four inches taller than him. I said, with a fake-sweet tone, "Nice to have met you. I'm sorry for not realizing that if I wanted to meet you and the friends in your support group I'd have to fuck you first. It was my mistake, so consider my application withdrawn."

Heidi and Mr. Married Guy had overheard everything – apparently Bill's whisper had been louder than I'd thought. Heidi was white as a ghost, and Mr. Married Guy seemed rather amused. Bill looked at me in shock, though I didn't understand how he could possibly be shocked after what he'd said to me. Had he been expecting me to apologize, send Heidi home and agree to sleep with him just because he was mad at me? He said nothing, turned and walked away. Heidi and Mr. Married Guy gave me a high-five and we spent the next few minutes speculating as to what medication Bill was on, or better yet what medication he *should* be on.

I never did find out whether Bill's support group was real, or whether it was just a front for getting laid. And I drove home that night with a mixture of adrenalin from the confrontation, and deep disappointment. I wondered whether I should give up on dating for a while, and focus on my kids and parties, in that order, instead. I knew I wouldn't – I was just too horny. But I couldn't help thinking that I should.

13
My Best Friend "Bob"

THOUGH MY DATING curve was more like a straight line pointing down into the ground, the toy parties were going nowhere but up. We were having no trouble scheduling at least one a week and sometimes more. We got referrals from friends, co-workers, and by word-of-mouth from people who had been to previous parties. Suddenly it seemed like our parties were the "thing to do." Everyone wanted in, and Heidi and I were more than happy to oblige, and to pocket a lot of cash along the way. (Note to the IRS: I reported every dollar I earned. EVERY dollar. I'm stupidly honest about stuff like that).

With all the experience I was gaining at these parties, I got very good at reading our partygoers. I did the same on a daily basis with my dental patients, and this was no different; people are people. I knew who could take a joke and who couldn't, who felt comfortable talking in public and whom I should allow to fade into the woodwork. And needless to say it was important that nobody feel they were being judged, whether by me, Heidi, or anyone else in the room. No matter what people said, I smiled. No matter what they asked, I treated it as a legitimate question and answered it as best I could. I learned to seem completely at ease talking about G spots, bondage, clits, and everything in between, as casually and comfortably as if I was describing a new kind of dental floss or my preferred brand of toothbrush.

That may sound pretty elementary, but trust me, it wasn't always easy. The more I did it, the easier it got. But every now and then, something – or someone – would throw me for a loop.

One of the parties I did was for a social acquaintance of mine. The party had a group of women from 25-45 years old. They were what we called "mixed," meaning both married and single. I knew the hostess and nobody else. (I had mixed feelings about that – there were times I felt more comfortable knowing the people in the room, though most of the time I felt more comfortable with a greater degree of anonymity). As usual I started with the most benign items, the novelties. For instance, we had an entire line of items for Bachelorette Parties, or as we called them, "penis parties." We had plates, silverware, candy, pasta, etc. in the shape of various body parts, plus some racy videos and even some anatomically-correct male blow-up dolls. These were easy to talk about because the partygoers could pretend they weren't serious about using them. They were "just for the party," even if some of the women harbored secret plans to put some of those things to use when they got home. My usual routine was to move and groove through those products until I could get to my real favorite, which was the big blow-up sheep with a penis on one side and a hole in the rear end for penetration.

This night was no different. I got plenty of giggles as I went through all the penis-parts, then I got to the sheep and held it up. But I learned a lesson that night – don't wear lipstick when blowing up the sheep! That's because the nozzle you blew on doubled as the sheep's penis. So right there on the sheep's penis, were my lipstick marks, for all to see. I was briefly thrown off balance, until I heard a voice from the audience. "Hey Heidi, nice job, I see you blow sheep. What else do you do?" I decided to ad lib, "Unfortunately on-line dating hasn't been going so well lately, so this was the best I could find." Although my statement had more truth to it than I wanted to admit, the partygoers had no way of knowing that. To them I was Heidi the sex-toy sales girl, cute, vivacious, with nice tits and a great smile. Obviously I was getting it day and night, right? So they all laughed, and started throwing orders at me. Which was just how it was supposed to work.

That was the easy part of the party. The sheep bit proved to be a great icebreaker. (I would eventually incorporate it into my routine, though I had to be careful not to do it too often, in case I had repeat partygoers). As I put the sheep away one of the older women yelled out, "Hey Heidi, you're cute and single. Is Bob the only man in your life?"

I was momentarily thrown for a loss. I had a good friend named Bob, who happened to be married to one of my best friends. What was she suggesting? I gave her a puzzled look and, a little bit worried, asked, "Bob who?" She then said, "Your Battery Operated Boyfriend!" I hadn't heard that term before, but liked it a lot. I confessed to my audience that "BOB" was, in fact, my close friend and one of the best lovers I'd ever had. It was perfect – it helped me sell more products and had the added benefit of being true. I told the "BOB" story at every party from then on.

As the night went on and the girls had a few drinks, the questions got increasingly personal and risqué. The talk turned to multiple orgasms, something that (sadly) many women have never experienced. I was talking about how good BOB was at helping get me there, when one of the younger women in the back yelled out, "Hey, Heidi, I don't think I've ever had even one organism!"

I thought at first she was making a joke, then I realized she was serious – not just about never having achieved an orgasm, but about thinking that what she was going for in bed was called an "organism." She was a heavy woman, with big, kind of droopy boobs and more than just a few tattoos; she looked like a hard-ass rider from a 1960s biker movie.

I responded, "Good, and I hope you never get an organism, though if you do they have antibiotics for that." Everyone laughed, and I was about to say I could help her try to achieve an orgasm. But before I could say anything she dug herself in even deeper, as she pointed to the "Decadent Indulgence" vibrator I was displaying and blurted out, "My man has a huge cock, but if I get one of THOSE things he'll get worried I don't think he's good enough for me."

That is actually a fairly common objection when women are considering sex toys – they worry about bruising their husband's or boyfriend's fragile male ego. For some reason it's okay for guys to look at porn or ogle the girls on beer commercials or at the beach, and we women are not supposed to be intimidated by the giant fake boobs and tiny waists we see all around us. But God forbid our boyfriends or husbands should see a vibrator in our nightstand drawer? Give me a break. Plus, isn't it a good thing to let our men worry whether they're pleasing us? Especially if they aren't pleasing us. I think a little bit of insecurity is a good thing. And if her man responds to that insecurity by running away, then screw him; she should find someone who cares about her pleasure and knows how to give it to her.

I wanted to say all that, and maybe I should have. But I felt these parties weren't the time or place for political statements. In an ideal world I wanted to tell this woman that she deserved as many orgasms as she could physically stand, and that if her boyfriend didn't like it that was his problem, not hers. But this was a commercial world, not an ideal one. So instead I said, "Okay, let's forget the vibrator and find something that can stimulate your clitoris during intercourse."

If I thought that was going to get me out of trouble, I was wrong. Motorcycle Mama wasn't letting me off the hook. When I mentioned her clitoris a bewildered look came over her face. Her upper lip curled up and she said, "You want me to find my r-i-t-o-r-o-u-s"? I couldn't believe it, this woman was a walking commercial for expanded sex education in schools! I exploded with, "No girlfriend, I want you to say C-L-I-T-O-R-I-S, because if you can't say it you sure as hell ain't gonna find it!"

There was a stunned moment of silence and then the room exploded with laughter, including her. In fact she seemed so at ease that I half worried she was going to ask me to help her find it. Not that I have anything against women taking care of their own, but if I were ever going to go that way it sure wasn't going to be with this one. But when she came up to me at the end of the party, it wasn't to ask me for sexual favors. Instead she bought $125 worth of lubes and clit stimulators and her friends quickly followed suit. So the party had a happy ending for me, and I could only hope that later that evening she had some happy endings of her own, not to mention ridding her sex life of any unwanted organisms.

At another party soon after that, I found myself in an extended discussion about some of our BDSM products. (For the uninitiated, "BDSM" referred to Bondage, Discipline, Sadism & Masochism. Though back then they were just called "S&M," a less accurate but more common term). In retrospect our BDSM product lines were pretty lame. Out of the more than 20,000 total products on our website, to my knowledge all we had for BDSM at first were one blindfold, a not-very-sturdy feather whip, a couple varieties of nipple clamps, one pair of handcuffs and a few sets of fur-lined wrist and ankle cuffs. But back then, even that limited product line seemed rather scandalous, and it wasn't that common for me to get questions about it. So I was less than fully prepared the night that one of my partygoers approached me and started asking questions about "ball whips."

She was an attractive woman, mid-to-late twenties, not wearing a wedding ring. She was looking over our products and seemed not to be finding what she wanted. I asked if I could help her. She said yes, and asked me whether we carried ball whips. I'd thought I'd heard it all, but this was a new one for me. Trying to sound genuinely interested – which wasn't hard because I really was – I said, "Ball whips? What are ball whips?" She said: "You know, things to whip a guy's balls, I like to make men cum by whipping their balls."

I'll confess that I had to struggle with myself. The sex toy salesperson in me was fascinated by what she had to say, and whether there was another product line we should be carrying. Just how many ball-whips might we be able to sell? But the woman in me felt horrified. I mean can you imagine the Internet dating profile? His would say; "I love a woman who has class, style, education, and who will whip my balls until I scream in pain and ecstasy." And hers would say; "I need a strong caring man who will happily explode when his testicles feel the sting of my whips and riding crops."

All of which was totally unfair, of course. We all have our little sexual peccadillos. Who is to say whose are right and whose are wrong? One person likes to have a finger stuck up his (or her) ass during intercourse, another person finds that totally disgusting. One guy likes to wear women's clothes during sex, another guy is horrified at the thought of it. Some women get turned on giving blow jobs, other women hate it. Some guys love cunnilingus, other guys find it gross. Who knows, maybe the world of Internet dating would actually be a better place if all that stuff were in our profiles, or if people who were fixing us up took that into account. Why bother even starting to date someone who is grossed out by the things that most turn you on?

And if what turns you on is whipping a guy's balls, what's wrong with that? Nothing, of course. And apparently this particular woman was thoroughly comfortable with it. So comfortable, in fact, that when she saw the look of puzzlement on my face, she excused herself, went out to her car, and returned with a sample of her own. It was a flogger with a long black handle, wrapped in leather, and a series of soft leather tentacles attached to the end. She said, "This is my old one. Do have you anything like this?" Unfortunately I didn't have any floggers with me, but I was surprised and pleased to discover we carried one on-line. I had found yet another piece from our product line that I needed to explore.

With experiences like that, our business, as well as my sexual IQ, grew by leaps and bounds. Our earnings, both per-party and per-person, seemed to go up with every event. But while my income grew and my debts shrank, I still headed for my bedroom each night waiting for someone to come along to replace my BOB.

14

The One-Hundred Man Challenge

I LOVE A good challenge. I knew this guy who was a movie critic and local TV celebrity. I think I assumed that since he was on TV he must know what he talks about, regardless of the subject. So I took him seriously when he offered me some friendly advice about dating. He said that I should be prepared to go out with at least one hundred different guys post-divorce before I'd meet The One. At the time I thought the idea sounded ridiculous. But I began counting anyway. And it didn't take long before I concluded it might be overly optimistic. I continued dating, and the number count of guys I started seeing started to rise, without much hint of success. Over one three-week period I went on seven dates with four different guys, all of whom I was introduced to through my patients. And let's just say that, though it was wonderful for my patients to think so much of me, as matchmakers they sucked. With very little conversation beforehand, I agreed to meet the first guy at a nearby bar for a glass of wine. Including all the guys I'd gone out with before I'd started counting, this was number twenty. A bit of a milestone, I suppose. And it did prove memorable, though not in a good way.

    I am of somewhat below-average height for a woman – 5'4 in flats – so I'm not accustomed to towering over my dates. But this guy was so short I could have breast-fed him standing up. My first thought when he came up to me and said hello was that I was going to have to lift him up onto the bar stool. He might have been five feet tall if he'd stood up really straight. I knew it was wrong for me to judge the book by the size of its cover, but I couldn't help finding him amusing, like a sitcom sketch where a woman meets a guy in a bar, accepts a date with him, and then discovers the guy is standing on a bar stool.

I will confess that the guy was a good talker. A bit too good, in fact. I opened up to him about some of my dating frustrations. This was a mistake because he apparently took this as his cue to let the floodgates open. I learned more about him in the next ten minutes than I would have wanted to learn in our first ten dates. Among the things I learned was that he was at a "crossroads" in his career (read, unemployed), and that back when he was still married to his now-ex-wife, she'd given him the crabs.

I decided to keep our date as short as possible (no pun intended). One glass of wine and out! That was the outcome from me agreeing to a date without talking to the guy first, so I decided to try a different approach. The next day I had a "screening" telephone conversation with another fix-up from a patient. The guy seemed normal at first. He'd been divorced for five years, owned his own home and had a real job. And no mention of sexually-transmitted parasites. Things were looking up. So we agreed to meet for a drink after work. I was about to tell him how he could recognize me, when he said, "Oh, you'll have no trouble recognizing me, I look like a troll."

To me, a troll is a little doll with long green hair coming out of the top of its head. This was not a pleasant thing to imagine about my date, so I took it as a joke. I ignored it and went on to give the usual description of myself – 5'4", with big, wild, blonde hair.

We were meeting at a restaurant which had a bar area that was up a flight of stairs. I walked in and immediately spotted him at the bottom of the steps. My god, he really did look like a troll! He wasn't much taller than the last guy. His face was wider than it was long, and his ears stuck out like the handles of a jug. His nose was low and broad, his eyes round and set far apart, his hair sticking straight up and wispy. If not for the music coming from the bar, I'd have thought he was standing under a bridge in some children's story. I was tempted to ask him if he was going to try to sell me some magic beans, or ask me to pay a toll to cross the stairs.

I tried to hide my amusement – and disappointment – as we made conversation at the bar. Unfortunately, what he lacked in looks he made up for by being a dull conversationalist. We spent the good part of an hour talking about school systems and hot lunches. Tater tots and hot dogs are not what I want to be talking about on a date. I got out of there at the first break in the conversation, before we could move on to baked beans and Sloppy Joes.

My date with Man #20 had lasted ninety minutes. My date with the troll ended after just sixty minutes. The next guy, Man #22, only made it to fifteen minutes. He'd sounded good on the phone, but when we met, the first thing I noticed was the sad, pained look on his face, as if someone important to him had just died. I said, "Hello, nice to meet you." He asked me what I'd like to drink, and I asked for my usual glass of Cabernet. His next question was, "Are you in menopause yet?"

I almost spit my wine out and left on the spot, but politeness got the better of me, although, in retrospect I'm not sure his question deserved any politeness. I spent the next ten minutes thinking up an excuse to leave. I finally came up with, "I'm sorry but this wine seems to be bothering my stomach, I really have to leave." I half expected him to ask whether I was having stomach problems due to menopause, though at that point I didn't care what he said. As I bolted to my car, it occurred to me that my BOB would never ask me such a stupid question.

No wonder dildos were so popular.

15
Out of the House

THE INITIAL SPLIT from my husband was deceptively easy. In a matter of just a few months we had filed for divorce, reached an agreement on the terms and sold (though not yet closed) on our house. We had agreed that my moving date would be six weeks later, which also happened to be tax day, April 15th. For a while I'd been tossing things out, a few things here and a few things there, trying to avoid any last-minute rush to pack up the kids. The last thing they needed was more disruption in their lives. And now I had a full six weeks to finish off the process. Everything seemed to be coming together.

That is, until a week later – Wednesday, February 28, to be precise – when a gas company rep called to confirm that the gas was being turned off on the following Monday, March 5. I asked her to double check the address, as it must have been a mistake. She put me on hold for what seemed like forever, subjecting me to music that would have been annoying under any circumstances, but even more annoying when played over and over again. Finally she returned to the phone and said yes, it was being turned off on Monday, and as of Tuesday the billing address would be listed in another person's name, a name I didn't even recognize. She asked me if we had sold our house. I said, yes, and that the transfer was scheduled for April. She told me I had better check on that because the account was to be terminated on March 5. When I started getting angry with her, she apologized, said there was nothing she could do for me, and hung up.

I left the kitchen and made a beeline for the den that doubled as our home office. My husband was OCD-like in his organization – everything always in its place. So I was immediately suspicious when not only the contract paperwork for our house sale, but the entire folder, was missing. Feeling a bit queasy, I started going through his personal calendar. On Saturday, March 3 – three days from today – I found the following entry: "moving truck 8 A.M."

Things were becoming clearer, though I was still trying to convince myself I must be misreading the signs. So I called my soon-to-be ex-husband at work, but he didn't answer. Not sure what else to do, I tracked down the name and phone number of the people who had bought our house. I immediately recognized their last name as the name the gas representative had given me. So I called them. The wife answered the phone. She was very friendly, and very excited about moving into their new home. I asked her when the closing was set for. She said title was going to transfer on March 5 and that they were moving in on the following Friday, March 10.

"What? I'm not moving until April 15."

She said, "That was the original transfer date, but we wanted to move earlier. So we called and negotiated new dates, and your husband initialed all the changes on the contract."

"What the hell are you talking about? I never initialed anything, this is my house until April 15, nobody is going anywhere until then!"

She was now sounding a little less friendly. "I'm sorry; this is between you and your husband, keep us out of it. We're moving in next week." And she hung up.

In retrospect my first call should have been to our lawyer, as there probably would have been legal grounds for voiding the changes to the contract. On the other hand, I did want out of the house, and wouldn't have wanted to risk the buyers backing out altogether. So, instead of calling the lawyer, I called a couple of friends of mine to vent. After several conversations and a couple of shots of vodka, I was ready to confront my husband. He had come home from work, at which time he confirmed that he'd changed the moving date, and reminded me that he would be taking all of the furniture.

As jarring as this sudden move would be for the kids, I decided that trying to keep living and dealing with my soon-to-be-ex-husband would be even worse. So I barely slept the next three days as we rushed to get ourselves packed. In the meantime, his moving truck came and carried away all of our furniture to his new apartment. The only pieces of furniture he left behind were the kids' beds. I was left with a house full of boxes and toys, an eight-year-old son and eleven-year-old daughter, one dog, and no place to even sit down except the floor.

Fortunately my friends had already started gathering the troops. In a matter of hours I had a houseful of people helping me pack. (Needless to say, I made sure I packed up my bedroom myself). We packed, boxed, and bagged everything, loaded a rental truck and moved my stuff around the corner to my soon-to-be new home. The sellers were a wonderful couple. They both had gone through divorces and were sympathetic to my situation. Our closing date had been set for the third week in April, which was supposed to coincide with the closing date on our house. Even though we hadn't closed yet, my sellers took pity on me and let me store my stuff in their basement until our April closing date.

I had been running mostly on adrenalin, coffee, and occasional badly-needed glasses of wine. I was too busy to feel much emotion until, while packing my son's toys, we accidentally broke a boat made of Lego blocks. It was a fabulous sailing ship that he'd spent weeks working on. My son fell apart just as the boat had. We sat on the floor and cried together. As we hugged I told him we were like the boat. Our lives felt broken but we would re-build them. And the rebuilt versions might even be bigger, better and stronger than the old ones.

I don't know whether he believed me, but at least he stopped crying. And that was fine because I wasn't even sure whether I believed it myself.

Meanwhile, one of my friends and her husband had agreed to let us move in with them until we could get into our new house. They had three kids and a dog. The addition of two more kids and another dog created mayhem, but it was good mayhem. We were there for five weeks but by the end I think they were actually sorry to see us go. I know we were sorry to be leaving. For the kids it had been like one big party. It helped them – and me – forget for a while about how screwed up our situation really was. And it taught me once and for all, how stupid it is to try to do everything yourself, when you have a wonderful group of friends willing and able to help. My divorce had threatened to put me flat on my face, but my friends had been there to catch me, like a real-life trust fall. What a blessing they had been, and not a day has gone by since when I haven't felt grateful for that blessing.

16
Moving In (or Trying to)

I KEPT THINKING things were finally going in the right direction. After five weeks at my friends' place I'd closed on my new home, and had moved our boxes in. All we needed was for my new furniture to be delivered. My new furniture was a gift from my parents, who in a fit of generosity and protectiveness, had purchased it after I'd freaked out and run away to Florida. The furniture store down there had been keeping it in storage ever since it had been purchased. I also had a couple of pieces of the kids' furniture in storage in Cleveland and was able to coordinate delivery of my new furniture from the store in Florida with my Cleveland stuff. Everything was on schedule. Or so I thought.

On delivery day I took the day off from work – it was painful to give up the money, but it was a lot more painful to sit and sleep on the floor. Both trucks were scheduled to arrive in the morning. The local movers came right on time with my kids' furniture, but the truck from Florida didn't show up. I called the moving company, but all I could get from them was that they would "check into it." Finally at 4 P.M. the store called back and told me that they'd made a "mistake" and that their truck had left Florida without my furniture. I felt a meltdown coming, but after everything else that had happened, there was nothing left to melt. So I remained calm as they assured me it would "definitely" be delivered to me in five days. Meanwhile I slept in my kids' beds, alternating between my son and my daughter.

For meals I borrowed a card table and chairs from one of my friends. The kids actually thought it was fun, especially the part about having their mom sleep in their room. I found it less fun than they did – sleeping in a twin bed with a kid tossing and turning was not very conducive to a good night's sleep. But it was only going to be five days, so I did my best to grin and bear it.

Finally my new delivery day came. Again, I took the day off of work. And again the morning and early afternoon passed with no delivery. This time instead of calling the moving company I called the furniture store directly. They said (what else), they would "check into it." An hour later their customer service department called me. The woman on the other end asked me if I was happy with my new furniture. It turned out she wasn't responding to my earlier inquiry, this was a routine "courtesy phone follow-up" regarding the delivery they thought had already been made. Was I satisfied? How did the delivery go?

I can't imagine ever wanting to work in customer service; who wants to get yelled at all day by unhappy customers? And it wouldn't surprise me if the woman I was talking to decided to make a career change after our conversation. I angrily and half-hysterically explained what had happened and demanded to know where the hell my furniture was. She promised me a return call within the hour. True to her word, she called, though she regretfully informed me that my furniture was still in Florida. She didn't even try to explain how this had happened, and at that point I didn't even care. I made a brief and unsuccessful attempt to breathe and count, and then I just let her have it. I screamed that my ass had blisters from sleeping on the floor for the past ten days, that I still hadn't received a stitch of furniture, and threw in a few more choice four-letter words. I asked her what the &#@!* she was going to do about it?

She apologized for the inconvenience and promised a delivery within the next week, which I'm sure is exactly what she'd have told me if I hadn't screamed and sworn at her. Lesson learned - shit happens and will keep happening whether you like it or not. So keep breathing and just deal with it.

In the middle of all this, I did my best to maintain at least the outward appearance of a normal life. I got the kids off to school each day, and I went to work, at least on the days I wasn't sitting home waiting for furniture that never came. I also tried to go out to lunch occasionally with my friends or co-workers. One day I went to lunch with a guy I knew, whose parents were friends of my parents. He'd been recently divorced, had heard what I was going through and suggested we have lunch. I thought it might be a nice opportunity for me to vent, and possibly to receive some assurance that maybe this craziness would end some day. Instead, I got to spend my lunch hearing stories about all the women he had slept with since his divorce. At first I thought he was telling me this as part of a pep-talk – "I'm having lots of great sex, and don't worry, some day you will, too." But when he suggested stopping by my house with a "care package," including a "nice bottle of wine," I began to suspect he wanted to provide more than just moral support.

I was desperate for support, companionship, and (yes) sex, so I tried to convince myself he was a legitimate prospect. He was taller than me, had a job, and didn't ask me about menopause. But then that physical appearance thing kept getting in the way. I know women aren't supposed to care that much about how a guy looks, that it's "what inside that matters." But I'm sorry, when it comes to sex I care what he looks like. And this guy looked more like a bulldog than a hunk. And once I got the image of a bulldog in my head, it was impossible to remove. Whenever he talked about the sex he'd been having, which was pretty much all he talked about, I imagined him doing it doggie style. But I was, indeed, desperate, so I agreed, against my better judgment, to let him come over with his care package. He showed up drunk, and tried sticking his tongue down my throat in front of my son. I threw him out, though I kept the wine. I figured I deserved it.

The weeks dragged by, the excuses kept coming, and the furniture didn't. A month after the originally scheduled delivery date, I finally called to cancel the order and demand my parents' money back. I guess I should have done that at the beginning, because within an hour I got a call from the company's president. If I had felt okay cutting loose on an underpaid customer service rep, you can imagine what I felt comfortable saying to this guy? I suspect this man had never heard a women use four-letter words in the creative ways I came up with. By the time I finished he was assuring me an "absolute" delivery date the following week plus a big refund check for my inconvenience. And sure enough, the furniture arrived when he said it would, and the check, too. I offered it to my parents, but of course they refused, telling me to spend it on "something nice for the kids." I bought some new lamps for their rooms and spent the rest on window treatments and kitchen utensils.

It's amazing what some curtains and an omelet pan will do for your state of mind. Plus, of course, sleeping by myself in my own queen-sized bed instead of on the floor or sharing a twin-bed with a snoring 8 year-old. I was feeling better already. I got started with some remodeling I'd planned, and much to my amazement the contractor who was doing the work actually seemed to be on target to finish the work on time. So even though my kitchen was still a mess of wiring, half-installed cupboards and unpainted walls, I was feeling very much at home. As if to emphasize the point, the girls at my office surprised me by announcing that they'd planned a housewarming party for me, though little did I know what they meant by "warming."

They told me to reserve the next Saturday night for them and to get rid of the kids. My mother was more than happy to take them. Keeping my Saturday open wasn't a problem since (as they well knew) I wasn't dating anyone and the sex toy party business had also slowed a bit in the face of all my moving-related obligations. So Saturday arrived, I vacuumed as much of the sawdust out of the house as I could, I put on something nice, and waited for my friends to arrive.

I waited for the doorbell to ring, but before it did I heard an odd sound coming from the front yard. It was a deep rumble, as if a large tractor-trailer truck was idling in front of my house. I poked my head out the front door, and was surprised to see a large tractor-trailer truck idling in front of my house. Even more surprisingly, they were unloading something very big onto my front lawn – large curved pieces of wood and fiberglass were strewn around the yard. I watched as some workmen set up a giant mobile hot tub and began to fill it, right there in my front yard. I was unsure what was going on and asked the truck driver whether he was sure he was at the right house. Of course he was – I didn't have a functioning kitchen, so my friends had figured they'd move the party to the front yard.

By the time the hot tub was set up, the party had arrived. My friends and co-workers piled out of their cars, shouting congratulations over my new home. As usual they were prepared – they'd brought their kitchenless and furniture-challenged friend coolers filled with food, Island drinks with little umbrellas, lawn chairs, and a sound system playing calypso music.

I could only imagine what my new neighbors thought: The sex-toy-selling divorcee next door has only been here a month and she's already hosting a hot tub party in her front yard. Needless to say, the Welcome Wagon never arrived, but with a hot tub in your front yard, who needs a Welcome Wagon?

17
The Sad Spring

HAVE YOU EVER heard a gunshot? They say a gunshot sounds like a firecracker, but to me it sounded like a gunshot. And what made it much worse was that I knew my dog, Gabby, was on the receiving end of the bullet.

My contractor was in the house when it happened. I was in my brand new home office, enjoying the sounds of my kitchen cabinets being installed. Somehow over the noise of his power tools, the contractor heard some screeching tires and a thump. He ran outside, ran back in to my office and breathlessly told me that Gabby, our five-year-old German short-haired pointer, had been hit by a car and it looked very bad. Our contractor had been working in our home so long it was as if he'd become part of the family, and he held onto me like a kindly uncle might as we walked outside. But before I even got out the front door, I heard the gunshot. At first I couldn't imagine what had happened; isn't it just in the movies where people shoot animals to put them out of their misery?

Apparently not, because the local police had just shot Gabby. I can't imagine how badly she must have been suffering for a suburban police officer to be convinced of the need to unholster his gun and shoot a dog. And I'm glad my imagination has failed me. Neither the police nor the contractor would let me look at Gabby, so at least I was spared that gory visual. All I knew was that Gabby was dead, and I had to figure out how to tell my kids.

I was a complete mess, crying to the point of being unintelligible, torn between my grief over Gabby and my fear of how my kids would take it. The only thing that could have made the situation worse would have been my almost-but-not-quite-ex-husband showing up and yelling at me.

Which, of course, is exactly what happened.

The contractor had alerted my parents, and a friend of mine had stopped by and learned what happened when he saw the police cars out front. Somehow the news got back to my ex-husband who, for whatever reason I didn't understand, decided to head over. He'd never seemed to me to have been particularly attached to Gabby, so I'd have thought he wouldn't care. But from the way he acted, you'd have thought this was a pet that he loved dearly since his early childhood, who I had just beaten and kicked to death in front of him just for fun.

Right there on my front lawn, in front of my friends, the contractor and the police, he confronted me and said it was my fault Gabby was dead. Though in an odd way, this proved almost a welcome distraction. We never did figure out how Gabby had gotten out, but I'd done everything I reasonably could to keep her in the yard, including installing an invisible fence. My ex's distress over the demise of a dog he never seemed to have cared about before would have been comical if it hadn't been playing out in front of the whole neighborhood. Instead it was surreal, and humiliating. My friends and the contractor eventually had to escort him off the property, before my stepfather, who'd also shown up, tried to beat the shit out of him.

My experience with Gabby's death had certain similarities to my divorce. There was a terrible sense of loss. I had to accept that whatever I had was never coming back. I had to break the news to the kids and re-experience the loss through their eyes. Some people were quick to point the finger at me, while the real culprits managed to skate by. It all seemed so unfair. Wasn't I the heroine in this story? But if I was, then why did I seem to be attracting all the bad luck and criticism?

It was hard not to wonder whether I did, in fact, deserve some of the blame my ex-husband and various wagging tongues at the supermarket were heaping on me. As time passed, though, I discovered the obvious. I was neither as bad a person as I blamed myself for being, nor as good a person that I fantasized that I was. I was a normal human being, more particularly a member of a specific subset of human beings known as the Single Working Mom. I had my good days and my bad days. I handled some of my challenges very well, and screwed up some of them, too. I had plenty of bad luck and setbacks, but had my share of good luck and happy developments, too. When you have the stomach flu, it can be hard to remember how it feels not to be nauseous. And once the nausea is gone, it's hard to remember just how bad it felt. My life was like that – the good times were very good, and when I was in the midst of them, the bad times seemed a distant faded memory, even if they'd just happened a week or two before. But on the bad days, like the day Gabby died and my ex-husband berated me about it on my front lawn, it seemed like the entire world was against me. I just needed to survive the moment, and wait for the good feelings to return.

Which they eventually did, though not before I had to go through the extreme unpleasantness of telling the kids that Gabby was dead. They cried and moaned about the unfairness of it all. I didn't have to pretend when I cried along with them and agreed how unfair the world was. But together we resolved that we weren't going to let this sidetrack our lives. The very next day we went to the pound and brought home a puppy.

Louie was a German short-haired pointer like Gabby had been, but a six-week old puppy instead of a five-year-old adult dog. Maybe he missed his mother because he kept pissing on my carpet, and instead of chewing on slippers or furniture like normal dogs, he chose to attack my bras and any pair of underwear he could get his teeth on. He also had an unfortunate tendency to leave my chewed-up bras around the house or even in the front yard, as I discovered one evening when one of my dates showed up at the front door with one of them in his hand, asking, "Is this yours?"

Louie lasted only six weeks. Call him "special," "challenged" or just plain old stupid, we eventually gave up. We told ourselves that he needed room to run, more than my small ranch house and postage-stamp sized yard could give him. We found him a good home out in the country, or what passes for the "country" in the Cleveland suburbs, and decided to live a canine-free lifestyle for a little while. But those six weeks with Louie had been all we'd needed; we missed Gabby, but no longer felt the desperate heartache that had beset us at first.

All of this left me wondering whether a six-week fling with a guy might help me through my divorce, just like our fling with Louie had helped us through Gabby's loss. If I were to find a guy to have a fling with, I resolved to insist that he not piss on the floor or carry my bras out to the front yard. Was that too much to ask for in a man?

18

My First Single Summer

WE ALL KNOW that men are attracted to women in uniforms, for instance, nurses, cocktail waitresses, and policewomen. I'd always suspected my dental scrubs fit the bill, but once word got out about that the hygienist in Room Three was going through a divorce and running a sex toy business on the side, I seemed to attract male patients as easily as a reality TV show attracts nutty would-be contestants. It seemed that hardly a day passed without a guy with excess plaque on his teeth either hitting on me, trying to fix me up with someone he knew, or both. I'm leaning over him, picking pieces of last night's dinner from between his molars, and he's fantasizing about my breasts. Men are strange animals, indeed. Any attempt at friendliness on my part seemed to be interpreted as an open invitation to sleep with me. I'd say, "You're doing a great job of flossing," and he'd say, "Yes, let's celebrate. Let's have dinner tonight." At the end of one cleaning with a patient who seemed particularly intrigued by what my scrubs were hiding, I leaned over to turn on the water, and asked him if he needed to rinse. He looked directly into my eyes, held his gaze there for a beat or two (he must have read somewhere that women like that) and said: "Now that I'm done breast feeding I'm doing great." He also suggested that business might skyrocket if I were to start offering topless teeth cleaning. I responded by asking why on earth he'd ever want to get his teeth cleaned with his shirt off? I don't know whether he just pretended to laugh, but at least he didn't try to ask me out after that.

Meanwhile, I resolutely turned down each of the many patients who asked me out. After my experience with guys like the Troll, I also started turning down fix-ups, whether they came from my patients or my co-workers. These folks seemed to think that any person who was breathing and didn't have a vagina was just my type. But I continued to hold out for something a little better.

One evening I was hanging out with some friends of mine, Rob and Annie. They were a married couple with three kids, a dog, and a seemingly endless supply of friends and acquaintances to fix me up with. I'd been saying no for a while, until they started giving me the hard sell on their friend who lived out of town but was coming in to visit in a few weeks. All they told me was that his name was Sam, he was originally from Cleveland but now lived in Chicago, he had two young kids and he was going through a divorce that sounded like it might have some similarities to mine. At first the fact that he lived out of town made the whole thing seem ridiculous – what was the point of meeting some guy who lived 350 miles away? But then it occurred to me that maybe the distance would provide some safety. If he turned out to be a bad guy, then I had the protection of several state lines between us. And if he was a good guy, well, what can ever be bad about meeting a good guy? So I told them they could give him my phone number.

He called a day or two later. I knew I liked him right away because the first thing he told me was that he'd reacted the same way I had – he'd been skeptical about getting fixed up on a date with someone who lived so far away. He seemed completely different from the guys I'd been meeting. He didn't ask to see pictures of me in a bathing suit – in fact, he didn't ask to see any pictures at all. He didn't sound like he was just looking for sex, and to the contrary, when it came up, admitted he hadn't had sex with anyone but his ex-wife in the past 12 years, and hadn't any sex at all for nearly two years. His divorce hadn't been his idea, actually he'd been in love with his wife even after she shocked him by telling him she wanted a divorce just eight months after their second child was born. But he'd finally come to grips with it, and was ready to move on.

Or so he had told himself, just like I told myself I was moving on despite wondering whether I really was. I could hear a lot of myself and my own emotions and insecurities as I listened to Sam. Like me he'd been doing some Internet dating and was able to share some funny and not-so-funny stories about the people he'd been meeting. My friends had assured me he was good-looking but I decided I didn't care. Even if he was another troll or frog or dwarf, I was convinced I was going to like him. But of course, when I learned he was on JDate I couldn't resist looking him up. I was pleasantly surprised at what I saw; a dark-haired guy, an inch or two taller than me, in good shape. One of his photos showed him out West somewhere on some kind of bike trip. He was wearing bike shorts, which I was sure was calculated on his part; he wanted women to know he had a good body. But I liked it that he wasn't in-your-face about it. He looked very relaxed in the photo, there was nice scenery behind him, and the best part was that he looked really, really happy.

I realized that I'd been meeting way too many fundamentally unhappy people. They were unhappy because they were divorced, angry at an ex-spouse, lonely, not getting enough sex, or all of the above. Sam certainly had plenty of reasons to be unhappy given what was going on his life, but what I heard in his voice and saw in his photo, was someone who deep down was a happy person who could appreciate the good things he had, despite any of the bad things going on at that particular moment. I found myself looking forward to his visit without the feeling of anxiety or dread that I'd been feeling for so many of my recent dates.

Another benefit of Sam's out-of-town status was that I could control what he did and did not know about me. My friends had promised not to say anything to him about Heidi's Passion. As far as he knew I was a full-time dental hygienist, single mom, and that was it. With most of the other guys I'd been meeting I hadn't cared, but for some reason this was different. For the first time I found myself feeling a bit insecure about my "sexpert" role. Maybe I was afraid that Sam would find it bizarre and write me off as an unserious person. Or maybe I liked that he seemed to be more interested in me as a companion and confidante than as a potential sex partner. I was afraid that would change once he learned that I owned a warehouse full of sex toys. But regardless of the reason, this was a new experience for me. And I couldn't help wondering whether my side business had been interfering in my dating more than I had realized.

The weeks dragged by, but finally the weekend of Sam's visit arrived. He was going to be spending some time with his relatives. He also had his kids with him, but he'd arranged for their grandparents to babysit on Saturday night so we could go out. This was the first Saturday night date I'd had in a long time and it already felt very different from all the Wednesday evening let's-meet-for-a-drink dates I'd been having. I was nervous and excited. But I also had a big toy party that Friday night, which I needed to get through first. Most women go on a date and then talk about sex; I was going to do exactly the opposite. I could only hope it would work out for the best.

19
Horny Hockey Moms

I WAS NOT expecting Friday's event to be an ordinary party. It was a party for the group that I affectionately referred to as the Crazy Hockey Moms, not that I've ever met any other type of hockey mom. At the suggestion of one of the player's moms I had held a party for a bunch of moms from my son's league. About half were from our home team, the others were from rival teams. Our kids may have been competitors, but for the moms it was all-for-one-and-one-for-all whenever the subject turned to sex toys. I'd made a pretty penny at our first party, and everyone had gotten drunk enough that they were ready to do it again at the next opportunity. This Friday was the next opportunity, so I had some idea what to expect, though I could only hope it wasn't as extreme as our last one. In that one, unlike my strictly commercial parties with people I didn't know, we started the party at a bar where we got warmed up with so many pitchers of margaritas that we were acting like a bunch of sailors who'd just come in from six months at sea. We closed down that place, plus another, even though in the Cleveland suburbs that's not as impressive an accomplishment as it might seem. We finished the night in the goalie's mom's hot tub. We had been out at a local bar and had gotten so loud they kicked us out. We all ran into her house and started ripping our clothes off and getting naked in her kitchen and running outside to the hot tub. Her older son was sleeping at a friend's, but her five-year-old son was home. Instead of worrying about our indiscretions, we just giggled about how funny it would be if he wandered out to find a bunch of naked women in his kitchen. It felt good to act like a bunch of naughty housewives on a reality TV show.

Eventually the party started thinning out. One of the remaining moms realized she'd forgotten her towel inside. But since everyone else was parading around naked, she just sauntered into the kitchen, only to run into the hostess' son, who'd woken up and wandered in. He'd come into the kitchen looking for his mom and was instead confronted by one of his neighbors in her birthday suit. Breasts, ass, pubes, nothing was left to his imagination. His actual mom was immediately called and came running in as the unknown naked woman wrapped herself in a towel. The kid said his head hurt, so his mom gave him a Tylenol and put him back to bed. Whether he'd already had the headache or it had been caused by the sight of his neighbor's giant naked breasts, was anyone's guess. Maybe we can ask his therapist in twenty years.

The next day the hostess called me to report she'd found several pairs of frozen underwear in her backyard, and that at breakfast her son had said, "I think I saw Mrs. Potash naked in our kitchen." She had told him he had a fever and was imagining things. All I could do was hope I was never called to testify as to what had really happened.

The memories of that night in the hot tub were still fresh in my mind as I wondered what new stories I'd be able to tell after this Friday night. It was going to be an unusually big party. Fifteen to twenty-five women was a typical contingent, but tonight we were going to have close to sixty. Great for sales volume but I couldn't help feeling nervous at the thought of being in front of that many women. Still, I'd learned that once I get going, the material pretty much sells itself, and I figured tonight would be no exception. After my usual intro about how the night would work, I launched straight into some of the good stuff. And tonight I started with cock rings.

A cock ring is just what it sounds like – it's a ring that goes around the base of the penis. Cock rings come in all different materials, from stretch rubber to plastic, leather, and even metal. Their purpose is to prolong erections; it's harder for a guy to orgasm with a ring on his cock, and it's also harder for the blood that flowed in to cause the erection to flow back out. So the cock ring acts like Viagra, but without the need for a prescription.

I'd assumed my customers would all understand the benefits of a prolonged erection, but to my surprise I got some questions about that. A few women said it was already hard enough to get their spouse to orgasm, why would they want to make it even harder?

I knew I would never want to be in a relationship with a guy who had trouble getting off with me, and I couldn't help wondering how many of these guys were having trouble orgasming with their wives because they were getting action on the side. But I didn't let on where my thoughts were going. Instead I took the opportunity to remind my partygoers of something that women have been forgetting about in bed for too long – sometimes you just need to look out for #1! If all a woman is worried about is getting her husband off as quickly as possible, what's in it for her? Physiologically and psychologically, a woman almost always needs more stimulation than a man to reach orgasm, so why not force her guy to wait the way we women have been waiting our whole lives? Plus it shouldn't be so hard to sell to the guy. What guy doesn't want to be able to brag about how long he can "keep it up?" Maybe a few guys would be shy about it but most would be happy to know his wife was telling all her friends about their great marathon sex sessions. Not to mention that when the guy finally has that delayed orgasm, he's going to discover that it's a whole lot bigger than before. Trust me that after a few sessions with a well-placed cock ring the guy will be SOLD.

That was my pitch, and it was a pretty successful one. It also allowed me to segue into lubricants, because not surprisingly, proper lubrication is a must for longer intercourse. (Some women are regular lubrication factories but most women need some help from time to time). We carried a wide range of lubricants. You could get them in various consistencies, flavors, and different chemical compositions, e.g. silicon-based, water-based, hypoallergenic, etc. You could even get some that heated or cooled the skin. As the lubes were passed I asked for a volunteer to try the cooling and heating "pleasure lubes" on their private areas. Judy, a tall outwardly-conservative brunette, who apparently had had just enough to drink, nervously volunteered after being egged on by a few of her friends. Judy was a financial type, a high-level manager of a financial division of a big national brokerage firm. She seemed like she'd be most comfortable in a boardroom in front of a bunch of men as they perused a series of graphs and pie charts. She seemed less comfortable in front of a bunch of more or less inebriated women, who were all staring at her and waiting to hear what, if anything, was happening between her legs.

I always thought it was kind of amazing that anyone ever volunteered for stuff like that. And yet someone always did, and more often than not it was the last person in the room I would have expected to say yes. It's as if they spent so much time pretending not to want it in real life, they couldn't wait to let their hair – or panties – down when given the chance.

Meanwhile Judy had gone to the bathroom to apply the menthol lube. She returned and stood in the front of the room, looking off into space. Her mind was clearly on what was going on down below, and her pelvis wiggled back and forth a few times. Finally, after about twenty or thirty seconds that seemed much longer than that, her nervousness seems to disappear. Her face broke into a smile, she giggled like a little girl and said, "It feels like I've got a York Peppermint Patty between my legs! It's a cool minty sensation... and I likey."

My entire inventory of 30 bottles of "pleasure lube" sold out that night. I gave Judy a free tube, fully expecting that she'd be become a repeat customer. And she did.

The party was such a success that a few of the women weren't ready for it to end. As Heidi and I were packing up our materials and the unsold inventory, of which there wasn't much, about a half dozen of the women made plans to go out dancing, and invited me and Heidi along. Heidi begged off but I said yes, partly because it seemed like good customer relations and partly because I couldn't resist the opportunity to meet men, Sam or no Sam. Heidi took most of the materials so I wouldn't have to risk leaving it out in the car, and the girls and I headed off to a nearby dance club known for its late hours, well-lit dance floor, and its extensive supply of horny divorced guys willing to buy drinks for a big group of unaccompanied women.

The club had three stories, each floor a different atmosphere and music. What all three floors had in common was that the music was very, very loud and the dance floors were crowded. The seven of us bought drinks but immediately put them on a table and headed out to the dance floor. We hadn't been dancing more than a minute or two when a well-dressed guy leaned over and whispered in my girlfriend Stacey's ear. I couldn't hear what he said but I assumed he was hitting on her, as Stacey, a nurse by vocation, is very attractive and never lacks for suitors. Still the look of shock on her face told me this was no ordinary pickup line.

He continued to stand next to her, swaying just enough not to look out of place on the dance floor, but not really dancing either. Stacey now had a quizzical look on her face, and she seemed to mouth "Really?" to the guy, who looked at me, smiled, and nodded to Stacey. I leaned over to ask Stacey what was up. Suddenly I felt a pair of arms around me and I was in a lip lock. For a moment I thought the guy had attacked me, but it was Stacey. She pulled me into her and kissed me, on the lips. She was putting some muscle and passion into it, and I was too surprised to either kiss back or push her away. So I let her kiss me. When she finally let go I looked at her, looked at the guy, looked around the dance floor, and discovered everyone was looking at us. Then the guy started applauding, followed by everyone else on the dance floor. I ran off to find my drink.

Stacey followed me, laughing. When she got to the table, she explained that the guy on the dance floor had offered her $300 if she and I would kiss. I asked her to repeat that — three hundred dollars, really? She said yes. I couldn't decide whether I was horrified or intrigued at the thought of a guy willing to pay that much money to see two random women make out on a dance floor. But when I asked Stacey for my share of the money, my suspicions were confirmed — the guy had scammed her. He'd paid her, but had come up $280 short. Twenty bucks! The whole thing was too funny to take seriously, but somewhere I couldn't help feeling that our kiss had been pretty damn good, and that it should have been worth more than $20. Maybe it would have been if we'd told the guy what we'd been doing the past few hours. Maybe even showed him a cock ring or two? Would that be considered prostitution? It might have been fun to find out, and lesson learned – next time I would be sure to demand the money up front.

In the meantime, I had just had my first-ever full-on, romantic kiss with another woman. To my surprise, it hadn't been half-bad. In fact it was pretty good. I assumed this would turn out to be nothing but a good story. It also seemed like a pretty good way to get warmed up for Sam. Our date was very much on my mind as I headed home, hoping that he was even half as a good a kisser as Stacey had turned out to be.

20
Meeting Sam

I GOT HOME from the dance club around 2 A.M., with my head still buzzing from the music and drinks. It felt like I'd only been asleep for about five minutes when my alarm woke me for work at 6 A.M. Saturday was usually a busy day in the dental office, and this day was no exception. I was exhausted, but was also running on adrenalin in anticipation of meeting Sam. This was unusual for me, and enough people commented on what a good mood I seemed to be in that I began to wonder whether I was setting myself up for some kind of letdown. But I was too tired to think that through, so I decided to just enjoy the feeing.

There was no way in hell I was going to let Sam see me in my scrubs. So the moment the last patient was out the door, I was out the door, too. I drove home as fast as the local speed traps would let me, stopping along the way to pick up some cheese and crudités. I got home, showered, and started rooting through my closet for something to wear. I'd come up with a few options in my head while at work, but none of them seemed right when I put them on. This was a new experience for me; I couldn't remember the last time I'd had any trouble deciding what to wear on a first date. It was a typically hot summer day, and on my fourth or fifth try I finally settled on a sundress. I did the best I could with my hair, which was its usually unruly self, especially in the humidity. I cranked up the AC, checked to make sure the white wine was properly chilled, and put out the food.

As a precaution I'd invited Rob and Annie to join us for the appetizer portion of the evening. Supposedly I'd done it to be polite, since they and Sam hadn't seen each other for a while, and I told them I'd feel guilty if my date with Sam interfered with an opportunity for them to see their old friend. But I wondered whether the real reason was my nerves. This was the first time I'd ever invited someone who'd fixed me up to come along on the first date. Though after some of my most recent miserable first-date experiences, maybe I should have started insisting on it.

Sam got there first. I answered the door and was surprised to discover that he looked better than his pictures. Definitely a first. He was about my height, with a slight frame, but he was muscular enough that I wasn't left feeling overly bulky like I sometimes am with smaller guys. He had dark olive skin, almost Middle Eastern dark. But his best features were his eyes. They were very big, and very dark. A rich brown, the kind that I loved to look at.

When he stepped through the door we hugged each other. It was the perfect hug. Long enough to convey warmth, affection, and held just a heartbeat longer than necessary, conveying a little bit of flirtation. But not so long as to feel inappropriately forward for two people who'd just met. It left me wanting more. Like I said, the perfect hug.

Sam had barely gotten through the doorway when Rob and Annie pulled up. I was already wishing I hadn't invited them. I didn't know whether Sam was just playing it cool, but he seemed genuinely happy to learn that I'd invited them. So I decided to play it the same way. But I did notice that when Sam hugged Rob and Annie hello, the hugs were noticeably shorter than the one he'd given me. I was glad to see that.

We stood in the kitchen a while, eating cheese and crackers and drinking wine. We eventually adjourned to the living room, but before long it was time to leave for dinner. Rob and Annie had other plans. We parted ways in the driveway. Rob and Annie's car pulled away as I got into the Sam's gray Audi sedan. He started the car, backed out of the driveway, and put on some music. The CD he chose to play floored me. It was "The Big Calm," an album by a British alternative group called Morcheeba. I was quite sure that nobody but me had ever heard of them. When I told him I loved that album, Sam seemed taken by surprise. He told me he'd heard it playing at a restaurant a few years back and had loved it enough to track it down and buy it. I was the first person he'd met who had ever heard of it. Though neither of us said so, it seemed like the universe was telling us we'd been meant to meet.

I'd made a reservation at my favorite dinner club. Our conversation seemed to flow naturally, more like old friends renewing a relationship than two people who'd just met. The club was crowded and loud, and as usual I surveyed the room to see if there was anyone there I knew. Without even realizing it, I'd developed the habit of looking for women who'd been at my parties, and preparing a response depending on the situation. For instance, my response to "I loved that dildo I got last night" will differ depending on whether I'm at the table with the girls from the office, a date, or my mother.

So I did my usual survey, and my heart stuck in my throat. My friend Cindy, who'd been at last night's hockey moms' party, as well as for my make-out session with Stacey, had just walked in and immediately spotted me. I knew Cindy well enough to know she was not going to be reserved. I briefly considered jumping up, running over to her and telling her to keep her mouth shut, but something about Sam told me I should just come clean. So I looked at him and said, "Get ready, a woman is about to walk up to our table and thank me for a really wild party last night." Sam seemed a bit confused. I guessed he was smart enough to know there was another piece to this story but he seemed willing to wait for me to volunteer it. Meanwhile, like clockwork, Cindy bebopped up to the table and said, "Awesome party last night! And I love the new you-know-what!" She winked and returned to her table. As Cindy jaunted away Sam tilted his head at me with a quizzical look and a smile, seeming to assume that an amusing explanation was on its way.

I took a big swig of my wine, and told him I was about to tell him something I'd never said to a date before. Sam seemed pleased, presumably because his assumption that this was going to be something entertaining had just been confirmed. He asked if he should have some more to drink first, and I told him that was probably a good idea. He downed his glass, smiled, and said, "Well?"

I said, "You know that I'm a dental hygienist, but I also have another job. I helped start a home sex toy party company. So during the day I clean teeth, but at night I sell sex toys."

I really had no idea what kind of reaction to expect. Shock? Insecurity? Embarrassment? Confusion? But what I didn't expect was the reaction I got. Sam gave me a cute little grin, smacked the table so hard the wine glasses almost spilled, and said, "Oh my God, I just won the fucking lottery!" I remained speechless as he poured each of us another glass of wine. His mind seemed to go elsewhere for a moment, so I anxiously asked him what he was thinking. He leaned forward, bringing his head close to me, speaking quietly so I had to lean in close to hear. He said, "Do you want to know the truth?" And in a conspiratorial whisper, Sam said, "I'm trying to imagine what Cindy's 'you-know-what' might be, and how it might feel to play with it together."

It was if Sam had plugged my spine into a wall outlet and turned on the current. I involuntarily shivered, in a most pleasing way. How long had it been since I'd had that feeling? Try never. I'm sure the food was quite good but frankly I don't remember a thing about it. In fact I remember nothing of the club after Sam's comment. I was ready for just about anything, and I just wanted to get there, fast.

The problem was, I didn't know how. It had been a long time – seventeen years or so – since I'd been with anyone other than my ex, so I was a bit out of practice. And notwithstanding Sam's forwardness, he had his own insecurities – he hadn't had sex with anyone other than his ex-wife for more than twelve years. It was the blind leading the blind, though maybe it was going to help that one of us had a night job selling the sexual equivalent of a service dog.

After dinner I just wanted to go back to my place, but I felt nervous about saying so. Sam seemed a bit nervous, too, and said that since it was such a nice night out, was there anyplace we could for a walk? It seemed a strange request at 11:00 on a Saturday night, but we ended up on a breakwall along Lake Erie. In retrospect it was a pretty good idea. It really was beautiful out, the moonlight was very romantic, and we ended up holding hands and kissing a bit. Sam confided that the last time he'd made out on a Lake Erie breakwall had been the fall of his junior year of high school, some 30 years earlier. He'd been very nervous back then, not really knowing what to do, and he admitted feeling the same way now. This made me feel better because I was feeling that way, too. In fact the whole evening had had a bit of a high schoolish air to it, with the fix-up, having to get rid of Rob and Annie, the awkward social encounter at the club, and our mutual romantic anxieties. And I finally decided that, like in high school, the girl would probably have to take the lead if anything was going to happen. So I suggested we get off the breakwall and go back to my house. Sam seemed relieved at the offer and quickly agreed.

    A twenty-minute drive and a couple of glasses of wine later, we were rolling around on my living room floor, and it took no more than five or ten minutes of that before we made it to my bedroom. And once we were in bed, well, let's just say that Sam and I were both enthusiastic and he was unexpectedly talented. It was good. Very, very, good. By the time he left, it was nearly 5 A.M. I didn't envy him the task of waking up in a few hours to take care of his kids, but I was too physically spent – and happy – to worry about that. I had the best night's sleep I'd had in a long time. It was a rare and precious gift – the sleep of a satisfied woman. I didn't know where this was going from here, but for the moment I was pretty happy being where I was.

21
Health is Everything

THE WEEK AFTER you meet and sleep with a new guy you really like is the worst possible time for a colitis flare-up. So naturally that's exactly what happened to me. For those of you who are lucky enough to be unfamiliar with it, colitis is a condition in which your large intestine becomes inflamed, leading to many very unpleasant symptoms including abdominal pain, diarrhea, bloody stools, fever and, well, need I go on? I'd been fighting it on and off for many years, but the medicine my doctor had given me had been controlling it, and I'd been mostly symptom-free for the past few years. But whether it was stress or unfortunate coincidence, my colitis decided to return just a few days after Sam's visit.

It's hard to do any sort of work, whether it's cleaning teeth or demonstrating dildos, when you're making panicked runs to the bathroom every five minutes. And given the nearly hand-to-mouth financial existence I was then leading, a week or two in bed was a luxury I couldn't afford. So when I admitted to my mom what was going on, she had me in her car on my way to the doctor that same day. I told the doctor I'd been good about taking my medicine; did this flare-up mean I needed new medicine? He asked a few questions about my stress levels and I admitted they were sky-high; as if my finances weren't bad enough, my ex had just become unemployed and had stopped sending even the meager checks I'd been getting. I was wound as tight as a boa constrictor around its next meal.

My doctor sighed. The good news and the bad news was that the problem had nothing to do with my medication. My colitis had almost certainly been exacerbated by stress. He told me that I needed to slow down, to somehow reduce my anxiety levels if I wanted to help control my colitis. But how I was supposed to do that? I was in a Catch-22; slowing down meant working less, which meant less money, which meant more stress. So in my life's equation, less stress led directly to less money, which led to more stress, which led to colitis, which led to being laid up from work, which led to less money and more stress.

My doctor just looked at me and shrugged his shoulders which I guess was appropriate. He was a doctor, not a financial advisor.

As I got into the car with my mom, I started crying. I was working three jobs, trying to keep the kids on the straight-and-narrow. It sometimes seemed I spent eight hours a day working, eight hours a day driving my kids around or negotiating with their teachers or caregivers, and the remaining eight hours trying to unsuccessfully wind down enough to get some sleep. I'd tried just about everything to give myself relief, including a few things that seemed to hold some hope of helping. This included a support group for abused spouses (I hadn't been physically abused but I felt that what I'd gone through was close enough to pass muster, and my fellow group members seemed to agree). I'd also started doing yoga, which I found very relaxing and was one of the few "ordinary" activities that I regularly looked forward to. I began to meditate as well and to search for an alternative, more holistic approach to managing my life.

The car ride home proved very beneficial. It wasn't because my mom gave me any revelations, but rather because I reached some decisions on my own by talking to myself while she listened sympathetically. (If men could only learn the art of listening sympathetically, they'd be so much more useful). My daughter had been pining to go to summer camp, which I'd been resisting even though she'd been going four years running. It was expensive and her Bat Mitzvah was coming just a few months after she'd be getting back. However, in that car ride I realized that camp would be the best thing not just for her, but also for me. There is a lot more than a fifty percent reduction in stress when you go from two kids to one – it's more like ninety percent, especially when you're sending off an increasingly-hormonal thirteen-year-old girl and leaving yourself only with a not-quite ten-year-old boy.

Not that life was entirely a bed of roses with him. He was continuing to struggle with the divorce. Like any boy he wanted to look up to his dad but even at ten he was old enough to see that his dad was not an ideal role model. I also did my best to filter out my negative feelings about his dad, but at times I was a less-than-perfect actress and he couldn't help but notice. Fortunately he had the outlet of sports, which by his choice consumed pretty much every waking minute of his existence. By day he was at a summer sports day camp, and he went to hockey and baseball practices on evenings and weekends. The great thing about bats, balls, hockey sticks and hockey pucks is that they never let a kid down. They're always there, they never yell or complain. Instead they do pretty much whatever what the kid wants them to do, thus giving the kid a sense of control. So whatever struggles my son was having, they gradually faded into the background noise of his practices and games.

With him occupied, I needed to find a way to occupy my daughter, hence the summer camp. And as to that, fortune smiled on me – after the car ride, my parents talked about it and called me to offer to pay for her summer camp. My pride had led me to turn down many of their offers of charity, but in this case, for the benefit of my daughter and for my own health, I gratefully accepted.

The next day I told my daughter she was going to summer camp, and then I told my son he was going to have me to himself for six weeks. Everyone was happy, and for the first time in over a week I was able to eat a meal without being chained to the bathroom. Excited by this little victory, I decided to take some of the money I saved on toilet paper, and buy myself something a set of worry beads and an extra yoga class. After divorcing my ex, was it possible I'd also finally signed a settlement agreement with my large intestine? I could only hope so.

22
A Voluptuous Radio Celebrity

THE WEEKS BEFORE my daughter left for camp filled me with a combination of anxiety and exhilaration. She needed to finish studying for her Bat Mitzvah and I had to attend to the details of the event, which seemed to multiply faster than spare coat hangers in the hall closet. Thanks to his newly-unemployed state, my ex's small monetary contributions to the event had dwindled to zero. This made it easier and harder – a smaller guest list meant easier logistics but also that I had to make hard decisions about who would and wouldn't be invited. The party was going to be a hayride and barn dance. I cut every corner I could find to ensure I'd be able to pay for it. I wanted to insulate my daughter as much as possible from the financial pinch I was feeling. One way or the other, the party would go on, and thanks to Heidi's Passion it would be possible. Dildos and Bat Mitzvahs – who would have thought?

When I wasn't talking to my daughter's Bat Mitzvah tutor, the temple office, or the party venue, I was working my multiple jobs, running parties, and trying to find a little time to "play" on the side. I was continuing to talk to Sam, but to my disappointment it seemed to be blossoming into more of a friendship than an ongoing romance. The geographic distance that had made him feel so safe was now making him unavailable. But maybe that wasn't such a bad thing, as the positive experience of that weekend had inspired me to start dating again. Still suspicious of my friends' or co-workers' taste in men, I decided to give Internet dating another try.

This time, though, I approached it with a new attitude. I stopped assessing each guy who wrote to me as a potential husband and feeling disappointed when he failed the test. Instead I viewed each message as an invitation to social interaction. I filtered out guys who were either too serious or not serious enough. I was able to enjoy the banter regardless of whether it was going anywhere. I carried on a several-day affair with a dentist from Florida. He offered to fly me down there to meet him and I told him I was considering the offer. I didn't care whether he was serious about it, and I chose not to care whether he cared if I was serious. I was having fun. It didn't hurt, of course, that we had our professions in common, not to mention that he was very good-looking and apparently had money. In the end I said no, without guilt. I'd never been that good at geography, but I was good enough to figure out that if Cleveland-to-Chicago hadn't worked with Sam, West Palm Beach wasn't going to work, either. Slowly but surely, I was learning.

I was drawn into a correspondence with another guy who turned out to be a radio talk show host in California. He was in his late fifties, which was outside the age range I'd put in my profile. That and his location would have normally led me to delete his message, but he asked me an intriguing question, "Are you fat?"

Okay, so maybe the question was more offensive than intriguing. Still, it seemed to beg for a response. In my profile I'd been offered several choices of vocabulary to describe my body type. I had chosen "voluptuous." At the time my 5'4" frame was tipping the scales at 140 pounds, not considered medically overweight, but certainly not slim or petite. As my grandmother would have said I was *zaftig,* which is Yiddish for "some meat on the bones." I was curvy with big boobs so when the profile template offered "voluptuous" as an option, I checked the box.

I assumed this guy wanted to know whether "voluptuous" actually meant "fat," so I wrote back, "What kind of obnoxious question is that?"

He responded by confirming that to him "voluptuous" was code for "fat." But he then said that my photos looked anything but. He said he wasn't coming on to me, that he had no interest in a cross-continent relationship, he was just fascinated by the way Internet dating forced us to develop categories for our body types.

I found that topic equally interesting. I wrote back that I couldn't control what men thought of when they heard "voluptuous." But to me voluptuousness is a state of mind. It's not just a body shape, but a body image. For so many years, whether it was the world of Sixteenth Century painters or 1950s pinups, a woman who was voluptuous was considered incredibly sexy. Think of Peter Paul Rubens' Century nudes (the source of the term "Rubenesque") or Marilyn Monroe in her heyday – voluptuousness was a good thing. And to me, it still was. If men thought that a few extra curves somehow made me fat or unattractive, then that was their problem, not mine.

Apparently my new pen pal thought this was a good answer, because he asked if I would mind doing a spot on that subject on his radio show. I thought, how can I say no? Women should speak up, and who knows, maybe some men might learn something.

We scheduled a time a few days later, and next thing I knew I was on the air. Going into it I was relieved that I didn't know any of my potential listeners in Southern California. At first I was nervous but my Internet "date" did a great job of easing me into it. Plus I'd spent so much time complaining to so many friends about the subject, that it proved pretty easy for me to talk about.

Soon I was responding not just to the radio host, but also to his callers. I wasn't surprised that one hundred percent of the female callers agreed with me. But I was pleasantly surprised to discover that some of the male callers took my side, too. The majority of those who didn't were younger guys who said they find thinner women more attractive because they look healthier. The toughest question I got was from a young guy who said, "Be honest, if you could choose, wouldn't you want to be thinner? And if that's true, then why is it wrong for me to choose to prefer a thin woman, too?"

What made this so hard was that he was right. In fact, his comment made me wonder whether I was being a bit of a hypocrite. Of course if I could choose any figure I wanted, I would choose "athletic" or "fit" or "toned" or "firm" over "curvaceous" or "curvy" or "full" or Rubenesque. I could shout to the heavens, as I was doing, that I loved my body, and beg men to love it, too. But if deep down I would really prefer a skinnier Me, then why was it wrong for the guys I was meeting to prefer a skinnier Someone Else?

This points up one of the biggest problems with Internet dating. I call it the Shopping Cart Effect. When a guy meets one woman, he can assess what he likes about her and what he doesn't like about her, and decide whether, on balance, this is someone he wants to pursue a relationship with. After all, nobody is perfect. Unfortunately, when a guy is on the Internet he's not just meeting one woman, he's meeting ten or forty or four hundred at a time. So if one woman has six of the ten qualities he's looking for, he doesn't have to think about how important those missing qualities are. Instead he can just move on and hope that among the other hundred women on the list, he'll find one that is just a little closer to perfect. And then if he finds one who has seven of the qualities he wants, should he hold out for eight? And so on.

I keep referring to guys, but of course many women do this, too. Or so my guy friends tell me, since I didn't do it myself. Or at least I didn't think I did. I didn't go into all this detail on the radio show. In fact, I didn't go into any of it. Instead, when the caller asked whether I wouldn't really prefer a thinner body, I sidestepped the whole thing, and stuck to the party line. "I'm totally happy with my body, and if a guy can't live with some extra curves, then I wish him luck but he's not for me anyway." And I added this little zinger: "And good luck to him ten years down the road when he's got a dicky do, and a bald head, and his wife decides to blow him off for her Swedish tennis instructor. What's good for the goose is good for the gander!" I don't know how the caller felt about that, but the host – and all the female callers after that – loved it. (And in case you're wondering what a "dicky do" is, it's when a man's stomach sticks out more than his dicky do).

I hung up the phone after being thanked profusely by the host. I felt great about myself. But that one caller's comments hit home. I immediately went online and opened my dating profile. I changed my body description from "Voluptuous " to "Average." If that's what it took to get myself into a few more shopping carts, then so be it. To hell with idealism, I wanted dates.

And I got dates. Though compared to Sam, they were pretty awful. In fact, compared to a night home alone eating Spaghetti O's, they were awful. In the next month I went on ten dates with guys I met on the Internet. The first one stuttered so badly I couldn't follow the conversation. I'd had a health teacher in seventh grade who stuttered, and when we were learning about sexually transmitted diseases he got up in front of the class and twisted his face going "GGGGGG-G G." Everyone was yelling "green, go, guess," until he finally yelled out "gonorrhea." I thought about that the entire time I was on this date. They were not the kinds of thoughts that made me feel romantic. Did that make me shallow? Maybe, but this was going nowhere.

My next date told me that he hated his children and didn't like being forced to spend time with them. I couldn't believe any parent could actually feel that way, much less talk about it on a first date. There was no second date.

Date number three was a workout fiend. He had a great body, which I was happy to see, but not after he started mentioning it again and again and again. Eventually when he made a muscle for me with his bicep and asked me to touch it and feel the ripple, I couldn't stand it. I told him, you like yourself so much YOU feel it, and I got up and left. The seven that followed were just as unpromising.

Apparently my talk-show expertise wasn't doing me much good in the real-life Internet dating circuit. It was time for a new strategy.

23

An Island Escape

BEFORE LONG, I stopped treating the online messages I received as serious intros to relationships. Instead they became entertainment for the entire office. Some of the messages were so funny that I forgot how disappointed I was that they weren't leading to actual dates. One man said he found me so attractive that he'd been moved to write a poem. The poem read, "When I look at you I go cuckoo for Cocoa Puffs." This seemed very romantic, to tell me I reminded him of breakfast cereal. I wonder whether that had worked with other women?

Another man wrote that I looked cute but that I seemed a bit stuck-up, was that true? It wasn't clear to me whether he was hoping I would say yes or no. Maybe he found stuck-up attractive. Or maybe he was a submissive who was looking for a woman to constantly remind him how much better she was than him. If so, it was a tempting offer, but I still turned it down.

By far the most common inquiry — I must have had a dozen or more — was whether I was into casual sex. Guys wanted to know whether we had to have a formal "date" before I would jump in the sack with them. Too bad for them, if they'd known about my side business they might have been willing to put up with a date, maybe even two. But they didn't know, and I didn't tell them. If a guy didn't have the patience to spend at least a few hours seducing me over dinner, he sure as heck wasn't going to have the patience that being a good lover requires. So they missed out, and I made sure none of them ever knew what they were missing.

Sam had that patience in droves. He'd spent a good hour giving me a full body massage that first night in bed, and I can assure you by the time he was done, I was ready for just about anything. I don't know why more guys don't understand that about women. An investment of just a little bit of time and attention will be returned tenfold. But so many guys are too blinded by their egos, or hard-ons, or both, to get that. And any guy whose first question in an on-line message is about casual sex, definitely falls in that category. They can go screw themselves, because I'm certainly not going to do it for them.

Sam was in a different category. Unfortunately, he was also turning out to be unavailable. He came back to town one more time, a few weeks after that first weekend. We had a great time together and the sex was even better than the first time around. But once he returned to Chicago, it was clear our relationship wasn't going anywhere. He assured me it was strictly a matter of geography – I had kids here, he had kids there, neither of us was going to move for many years, so what was the point of developing a relationship? I was pretty sure there was more to it than just that. He was freshly (and painfully) divorced and was understandably fearful of getting into something new. So maybe the geography thing was just an excuse for a case of commitment-phobia.

But even if it was, I was appreciative that he seemed to care about letting me down easy. And it was probably for the best anyway, since I'd always been told, and have since come to believe, that nobody who goes through a "bad" divorce (and as we all know there are a lot more bad ones than good ones) isn't really emotionally healthy again until a good three years have passed. And neither Sam nor I was anywhere near the three-year mark.

So instead we continued to talk regularly. When he went out on a couple of dates in Chicago he called me for advice, and I did the same with some of mine. As a show of moral support, I sent him one of my favorite male products, the "Virtual Pussy." The Virtual Pussy was a roughly eight-inch long latex tube, which when properly lubricated gets very wet and squishy, to resemble a vagina. The manufacturer bragged on the back of the box that its product was "indestructible." Sam called me to complain a few weeks later that the Virtual Pussy had been very pleasing to use, but had proved anything but indestructible. I didn't know whether he was just kidding or not, but I sent him a new one anyway, and passed the complaint on to my product supplier, who cheerfully sent me a new supply. When you're in the sex toy business, "Keep the customer happy" takes on a whole new meaning!

But aside from my roles as Sam's pleasure facilitator and supplier of endless email amusement to my co-workers, I needed something to do. Working all of the time was wearing on me. I needed some fun.

One of the hygienists had a house on a small island in Lake Erie. With her husband's permission, she offered a getaway weekend for the office staff at the house. Taking a weekend off was a big deal for me – no work in the dental office, plus no parties, meant a big loss of income. Still, this weekend sounded far too good to pass up.

One very cool thing about the island we were going to was that you couldn't drive there. The only way to get there was either by ferry or a small six-seater plane. I opted for the ferry, as it was much less expensive and seemed a bit safer than the flight. Several of the staff joined me on the ferry, and the party began almost as soon as we left the dock. One of the young assistants made a rum concoction and started playing some great reggae music. We drank, danced and laughed for the full ninety-minute trip. We even met some adorable guys that partied with us. For the first time in a long while, I felt young, free, and ready for a great weekend.

24
What's a MILF?

MY DENTAL OFFICE was both tight-knit and very diverse, like a sweater stitched together from a bunch of different fabrics with patches on top of that. And if you'd judged us from our receptionist, it would have been a very, very tight sweater. She ran the front desk, checking patients in and taking phone calls. She was also a complete knockout. She had a fabulous body to begin with – long legs, a small waist, and a killer smile, topped by blonde hair that just wouldn't stop. And she liked to adorn herself in designer clothes, shoes, handbags, false eyelashes, you name it. I was never sure where she got the money for that stuff, though I speculated that perhaps our dentist was secretly giving her bonuses, since it sometimes seemed that half of our male patients came just to see her. When I asked how she could afford all that stuff on a dental receptionist's salary she just smiled. I could appreciate her secretiveness given my secondary line of work, so I just smiled and admired her amazing legs, just like everyone else did.

At the other end of the spectrum was a matronly woman in her 40s who behaved as if she was in her 60s, though in a happy grandmotherly sort of way. She was our insurance expert, handling all the patients' forms and maneuvering through the bewildering thicket of insurance minutia that seemed to come up on nearly every claim. She had the smallest, yet most involved family I'd ever met. It sometimes seemed she received dozens of calls a day from various relatives, seeking advice, offering advice, or just calling to say hello. Maybe she was really a bookie and if so it was a brilliant cover; nobody thought twice when she slipped away to take yet another personal call, and another, and another. Come to think of it, maybe she was actually pimping for the receptionist? If it was true, I wanted in on the action.

There were six other women in the office – three dental assistants, one more front office girl, and one more dental hygienist. Most patients didn't understand the difference. The assistants helped the dentist in all of the procedures, sterilized instruments, set patients up in the room, took x-rays, and became jacks-of-all-trades in the clinical area. The hygienists did all that, too, but also cleaned teeth, took patient histories, and removed sutures, among other things. The assistants tended to be younger, had high-school diplomas, and earned around $12-18 per hour. The hygienists, including me, had a Bachelor or Associate's degree in Dental Hygiene, and earned more than double what the assistants did.

The assistants also had more fun. Or so it seemed at the time. They loved to brag about their sex lives, and if even half of what they claimed they were doing was true, they had every right to brag. One of the front office girls was a lesbian, and proud of it. And it sounded like she was getting the best sex of all. Occasionally while listening to her go on about her latest exploits, my mind would drift back to my girl-on-girl kiss with Stacey on the dance floor. Sam had confided to me that for a while during his divorce he'd been so unhappy that he'd considered becoming gay just to make a statement about how fed up he was with women. Which made me wonder, might I be better off with a female lover? I'd always thought I was joking when I complained that sex was so much fun, it was too bad it required a man to do it. But seeing this cute, perky twenty-something bouncing around the office, I couldn't help but wonder what this upcoming weekend away might bring.

The first night we turned up for a fish fry at a local restaurant. There were twenty-three of us in our group. The twelve from our office included a few boyfriends and the dentist, plus a few tag-alongs and hangers-on, most of whom I didn't know. They weren't all single, but for this weekend they were behaving as if they were all available.

The restaurant had a small eating area with barely enough tables to accommodate our group. We took up probably three-quarters or more of the restaurant. The décor was sparse and had, not surprisingly, a marine theme, with cheesy tablecloths with anchors on them, and the requisite ship's steering wheel on the wall. Off to the side was a bar area, which was larger than the restaurant area. That wasn't a good sign for the quality of the food, which turned out to consist largely of fried cheese sticks and french fries. The white wine I ordered tasted pretty bad, but it was cheap and contained alcohol, which was all I really cared about. And in any event it wasn't the food, drink or even the people I'd arrived with that would soon make the evening so memorable.

There were a couple of pool tables by the bar. I took a break from my fried cheese sticks to go shoot some pool. I took my bad wine with me, got the bartender's attention, and gave him a couple of dollars to change into quarters. I noticed a couple of guys who really didn't look old enough to be drinking checking me out. I gave them the same smile I might have given to a couple of my son's friends at a hockey game (I call it my "friendly, cool Mom look"). I walked over to the pool table, bent over, put the quarters in, and gave a pull. The balls came out, and I started to rack them up, again having to bend over the table to do it. The assistant I was playing with then gave me a quick elbow, and motioned over to the bar. The guys I'd smiled at were still looking at me, and when they saw me look over they gave me a thumbs-up, and one of them called over, saying, in exaggerated mouth movements, "Nice tits!"

I just stared back in surprise, wondering whether he could really be talking to me? My companion was in stitches so I decided to go along, and I smiled and mouthed back, in the same exaggerated way, "Thank you!" The guy who'd made the "nice tits" comment immediately jumped up off his barstool and came over. He wasn't bad looking, if I ignored the fact that I was old enough to be his mother. I thought I was in for an extended conversation, or that he was going to challenge me to a game of pool. But instead he just came up, raised his beer glass to me, and said, "You're a real MILF," as he walked by toward the bathrooms. Had he said "milf?" Or was it spelled "milph?" Or maybe he'd actually said milk? I had no idea what he was talking about but he'd made it sound like a compliment, so I shouted "Thank you, I think" to his back. I returned to my game of pool. A few minutes later, apparently having completed his business in the men's room, he came back, and as he walked by he whispered "MILF" in my ear, gave me an overly confidant, mostly drunken grin, went back to his friends at the bar, and got high-fives all around.

These days, everyone knows what a "MILF" is, or so it seems. But back then it was a new term to me.

Convinced I was supposed to know what a MILF was, I became worried that I was being made fun of without realizing it. With a rising sense of paranoia I abandoned the billiards table and went back to our group. I didn't even bother talking to my fellow "old" people. Instead I went straight to the assistants and asked them what a MILF was? They started laughing and asked why I wanted to know? When I explained, they all started checking out the guys at the bar and were in hysterics. Fortunately my bad wine had kicked in, so I was able to have fun being the apparent butt of everyone's laughter. They decided to poll the entire bar. They dragged me over and one by one, started presenting me to various guys and asking them if they thought I was a MILF. Nobody asked them what they meant, as apparently everyone in the world but me knew what a MILF was.

The consensus in the bar was that I was definitely a MILF. I was having fun with it at this point – my vow not to think about men this weekend had long since gone out the window, and I was enjoying being paraded around the bar, being sized up – apparently favorably – by all the men there. And I had just decided that maybe I was never going to find out what a MILF was, until one of the guys my girlfriends polled, answered with, "Yeah, I'd definitely fuck her." My eyes widened, and one of the assistants, figuring the game was up, whispered in my ear, "MILF means 'Mother I'd Like to Fuck.'" I pretended to be horrified, which in part I was. But I was also enjoying the thought of the dozens of guys in that bar, all saying they wanted to have sex with me. Was it really true they all wanted to fuck me? Damn!

It was an intriguing thought. And when I went to bed that night – alone, unfortunately – I was very sorry I'd left my vibrator at home.

The next morning I woke up early. Thankfully the wine had been so bad that I'd been unable to drink more than a couple of glasses, which saved me from the hangovers most of my housemates were suffering. The house we were staying in had three bedrooms, plus three extra rooms with mattresses, cots, and sofas. There were also three tents set up in the backyard, one of which I had happily moved into. As the sky brightened I felt increasingly awake, so I threw on some sweats and went for a quick little walk along the lake. It was beautifully tranquil. I was alone, except for some guy walking up the beach in my general direction, who I happily ignored. I found myself feeling that maybe the world wasn't such a bad place after all. It was a feeling that had been all too rare lately.

The chilly sunrise air started working its way into my sweats, so I headed back to my tent. The guy walking up the beach was now only about ten to fifteen feet behind me. He was pretty buff-looking in a pair of jeans and a black t-shirt, like he had just come off the stage after winning a Bruce Springsteen look-alike contest. He gave me a little hello-wave when he saw me looking his way. I waved back but paid him no more attention because, in addition to looking very buff, he looked very young, maybe his late 20s. I climbed into my tent, and started rooting around for whatever self-help paperback I was reading at the time.

I heard the gentle tap, tap, tap of raindrops on the tent. It didn't bother me, of course. I rather liked the idea of being safe and dry in my tent while the rain fell outside; it's one of the best tent experiences one could ask for.

Or was it? Within a minute or two, just as I found a book and started getting myself into a comfortable reading position, someone said "knock-knock." The voice was unmistakably meant for me, as it was coming from immediately outside my tent. Although the tent was a one-person tent, it was big enough to stand up in, for which I was grateful when I opened the flap to find the guy from the beach. He introduced himself as Josh, and asked if he could come in to get out of the rain for a few minutes. He wasn't particularly wet yet but the rain was starting to come down harder. Maybe it was silly to feel safe, but I did with my friends' tents so close by. Plus it was 7 on a Saturday morning. Bad things don't happen that early on a Saturday, do they? So I said yes, and he crawled through the flaps.

Close up I couldn't help noticing more clearly what I'd already seen out on the beach. He was really good-looking. And really, really young. He had dark brown hair, on the longish side, and a beard which on an older guy would have looked like unkempt stubble, but on him looked pretty darn sexy. I'd guessed his age at late 20s on the beach; in here I figured 28 at the most, and probably younger than that. I wanted to ask but didn't, maybe because I really didn't want to know.

We talked for a while about nothing in particular. He was from Toledo, worked in an auto repair shop, and was up for the weekend with a few of his buddies, just camping out and drinking beer. I learned he'd been at the same bar as us the night before. He also had good teeth – something I've always considered a non-negotiable in a guy. I might be willing to start dating a guy with bad teeth, but if the relationship is going to go anywhere, he's going to have to get his teeth fixed. And this guy's teeth had no need of fixing, they were perfectly aligned and perfectly white, a combination I attributed to braces as a teenager and (probably) good genes. They also told me he didn't smoke, which was a good thing. Against my better judgment I found myself feeling attracted to him.

I'm not sure whether he was a mind reader or had planned it all along, but at almost the precise moment I decided I found him attractive, he took his shirt off. Just like that I was in a tent with a shirtless, good-looking twenty-something auto mechanic. He had less body hair than I would have expected, and bigger muscles than I'd have thought a guy of his size could have. But all I could bring myself to say, was, "What are you doing?" He said, my shirt was kind of wet and uncomfortable, plus I thought we could, maybe, you know, for a while?" And he leaned over as if to kiss me.

In my fantasies I would have fallen into his arms, kissed him passionately and then proceeded to fuck our mutual brains out. The fact that my girlfriends' tents were so close by would have added to the excitement. And the coupe de grace would have been them seeing him crawling out of my tent a few hours later, this cute young hunk, with a satisfied grin on his face, thanking me for such a great time. And I'd have spent the rest of the weekend in a happy, post-orgasmic haze.

I let him kiss me for a few moments of bliss, then reality hit and I pushed him away, scurried as far to the other end of my sleeping bag as the tent would let me, and asked again, "What are you DOING?" He said, "Well, when you invited me into your tent, I just assumed you might wanted to hook up? Sorry if I was wrong." A sulky look started to come over him as he reached for his shirt, and against all reason I started feeling guilty for hurting his feelings. I told him I was really flattered that he wanted to "hook up" with me. I told him he was a really good-looking guy, and that maybe if it wasn't 7 on a Saturday morning with all my friends around, he could have talked me into it. But it wasn't going to happen this morning. Conveniently the rain had subsided, so I suggested maybe he should be getting back to his friends, and that he should feel free to tell them the story about how he hooked up with a MILF who let him into her tent on the beach. He laughed and after putting his shirt on, asked whether we could kiss, just once more, so he wouldn't have to be totally lying. I said sure, why not? As we kissed he started pressing against me, clearly making another play, and I gently pushed his body off mine. He accepted this additional rejection with another smile, and just like that he was out of the tent and gone.

I could still feel his lips on mine and wondered whether I'd done the right thing. Maybe some quick, casual sex with a twenty-eight year-old (or whatever) stud was just what I'd needed? But even without that, I'd gotten some of what I'd needed anyway – a huge boost to my self-image. In the last twenty-four hours I'd been ogled and pursued by a pretty wide assortment of men, all of whom said they wanted to go to bed with me. Under other circumstances I might have felt depressed that none of them wanted relationships, all they wanted was sex. But under these circumstances it made me feel good about myself. You know that "glow" you sometimes see in people who've been having really great sex? Well, I'd gotten the glow, but without the sex. I spent the rest of the trip (which was too uneventful to write about here) with a smile on my face. I stood up a little straighter, paid a little more attention to my hair and clothes, and at the docks flirted shamelessly with the boat captain, so effectively that he actually chose to pay attention to me over our bombshell receptionist. When I got home, my mother, kids and several of my patients commented over the next few days how happy I seemed. And they were right, for the first time in quite a while I felt good about the world and my place in it.

But when they asked what had happened to put myself in such a good frame of mind, I chose not to tell them. What happens in my tent, stays in my tent.

25
Too Good to Be True

IT SEEMED THAT every guy I dated had some fatal flaw. No matter how many good qualities they had, there was always something that made them undateable. For instance, I got introduced to one guy through a friend of a friend. He seemed okay at first, not bad-looking, and a decent conversationalist, even if he did seem a bit obsessed with explaining just how BIG a house he'd lived in before his divorce. But he was good enough to get a second date, at which point he segued from telling me how big his first house had been, to telling me how small his current apartment was. He said he'd been surprised to discover that he preferred the much smaller space, because there was so much less stuff to keep track of. Since my own divorce had forced me to give up many of my most materialistic fantasies, I felt I could relate to what he was saying. And when, after dinner and a couple of drinks, he suggested I come to his apartment "to see what it's possible to do with small spaces," I decided to let myself fall for the line.

As he put the key in the door, he turned to me and said, "Oh by the way, I have a few pets." A few? I walked through the door and I almost staggered from the smell of urine. I felt queasy and wanted to sit down until I saw where I'd be sitting. The room was littered with litter boxes. To my amazement there was even one on the couch. All told the guy had three birds, two cats, a ferret and some other animal I couldn't identify that he let ran amok in the place. He told me he didn't like to keep them in cages, but "most of them" were litter-box trained. I was surprised that the animals didn't eat each other, not that I knew – or really want to know – what ferrets eat. He took the litter box off the couch and said, "Sit down, I'll get us some wine, what kind of music would you like on?" I told him the truth, I wasn't feeling that well and needed to go. I tactfully just said, "Thanks for dinner." And I resolved that if I ended up having to buy flea and tick shampoo, I was sending him the damn bill.

Every time I had a dating experience like that, I would start to feel discouraged and swear off dating for a while. But then the memory would fade, I'd start to feel the itch again, and I'd accept a date, starting the cycle anew. On, off, on, off. I was counting, I told myself I needed to hit at least one hundred before I met my prince. And then I met Bruce.

My friends Steve and Linda invited us over for a cookout with, as she described it, "just a few people from the neighborhood." My daughter was away at camp so it was just me and my son. We arrived in our usual high-energy fashion, with armfuls of food. I love to cook, so every opportunity I have I go slightly crazy. In this instance I'd made two side dishes and a dessert. I was moving so fast on my way in that I almost dumped the giant bowl of potato salad I was carrying into Steve's lap. But I got it safely onto the counter. I then heard some little voice yelling for help from the basement. Nobody else seemed to notice, so I walked down the steps and found an adorable little girl named Sara who looked about three or four years old. She was trying to reach a box of toys high on a shelf. I didn't have time to wonder who she belonged to because the box was about to fall on her head. The box had a variety of odds and ends that appealed to her, but she immediately went for the various clown paraphernalia from some long-ago carnival or something. I couldn't resist joining in. We traded floppy shoes, beanie hats, Elton John sunglasses, you name it. We were very proud of ourselves and I suggested a "parade" to impress the adults upstairs.

Without even realizing it I found myself holding hands with Sara, for whom the railing was at a challenging height. We got to the top of the stairs and headed into the living room. As we carried the box outside a man I didn't recognize came up to me, looked down at Sara, back at me, and exclaimed, "I don't know you, but I think I love you!" Then he gave me a bear hug, and identified himself as Bruce, aka Sara's father. He was very cute, and had a great smile. His clothes and hair were a bit disheveled, as if he'd rushed to get out the door – a look I often have myself. He seemed very relaxed and I loved that he'd been confident enough to hug a woman he didn't even know, and more important, to do it without seeming the least bit creepy. I instantly liked him.

He and I joined the big group of kids out in the backyard. Bruce's other daughter, who was six, was also there, and she was as cute and fun as Sara. But it turned out that Bruce was the biggest child of all, and all the kids, including my son, loved him for it. As did I. He joined in when I got on the trampoline with the kids, and later crawled across the lawn with me as I helped the kids search for ladybug food. (A silly endeavor since none of us really had any idea what ladybugs like to eat). I spent most of the cookout hanging out with Bruce and chasing our respective kids around. When I left I was tempted to ask whether I'd see him again, but with all the kids around it didn't feel natural. So I just said good night, it was great meeting you, and my son and I got in the car and drove away.

The drive provided the first quiet moments of the night, but my son quickly broke the quiet and said to me, "I liked Bruce, and he liked you Mom, I think you guys are going to get married." I laughed. "Good thinking, but just one problem, he didn't even ask for my phone number." I tried to hide my disappointment when I said it. My son just smiled, and with all the wisdom of a ten-year-old could muster, he smiled and said, "I'll bet you he's going to call you for a date." We bet a dollar on it.

It was a bet I was very happy to lose. The next day I was vacuuming my living room when, over the roar of the ancient canister model I couldn't bring myself to replace, I thought I heard the phone ringing. I shut off the vacuum and ran to get it. The voice on the other end said, "Hi Heidi, this is Bruce. It isn't often I meet someone who blows me out of the water. You blew me out of the water, I couldn't stop thinking about you all day. I'd love to see you again." This guy was good. I had dinner plans that night but I asked him whether he'd want to come by after dinner and take a walk, seeing as how it was a full moon. I hesitated only because I wasn't sure what one wears for a first-date moonlit walk. He said, "Tell you what, why don't you call me after dinner and see if you're up for it?" We left it at that and I went back to my vacuuming.

When Bruce had first asked me out I'd tried to make my "yes" sound more casual than it really was. I didn't want him to know that I was reliving that feeling I used to have in high school upon learning that the boy I had a crush on liked me back. After dinner I called him as promised, and he came over for our walk. We walked around my neighborhood, which was fairly dark with widely spaced houses and large, mature trees filing in most of the spaces. The moonlight filtered through just enough for us to see where we were going. The combination of the speckled moonlight on the big expensively-manicured lawns, the chirping of the crickets and Bruce's childlike grin and relaxed confidence, couldn't possibly have been more romantic. I don't know when we started holding hands but it felt as if it was the most natural thing in the world. As the walk came to a close I asked if he wanted to join me for a glass of wine.

He followed me into the kitchen as I pulled out a bottle of wine and searched for a corkscrew. He put his hands on my shoulders, gently turned me around and kissed me. It was our first kiss but we might as well have done it many times before because it felt completely familiar and easy. I was so exhilarated that the butterflies in my stomach started hinting of fear. I just wasn't sure I was ready to feel anything for a man. We had a couple of glasses, we kissed a bit, and I started getting increasingly nervous. It's not that he wasn't good – he was too good. I truthfully told him I had to get up early for work the next morning. He left graciously with a long kiss and a promise to call me.

As I prepared for bed the voices in my head started to turn Bruce from a hero into a fiend. This guy was too smooth, they told me. Obviously he's a player, he's going to do and say whatever is necessary to get me into bed with him, and only then will I discover the real him. Don't let him get into your head, they said, which was ironic since if it was okay for these voices to be there, why couldn't he be in there, too? But I didn't think about that. Instead I told myself, yes, he's obviously a player. And I felt better as I started to write him off. After all, if I had no expectations from him, he couldn't let me down. Right?

But if he was just a player, he was so good at it that he was able to plow right through my defenses. The next day he called me and was so kind and funny and sweet and charming that I was ready to leave work, head straight to his house and give him whatever he wanted. But this time he was the one with previous dinner plans, so he suggested we meet after. We agreed, and when he came over we picked up right where we'd left off. And as if he knew I was worried about his intentions, he made no effort to get me into bed that night. Instead we just sat and talked about everything imaginable, from our divorces, raising children, and families, to our careers, anxieties, and pretty much everything in between.

Bruce made a point to say to me no matter how busy we get in our lives let's promise to make time to see each other. I was skeptical but agreed. I still had many fears. What I didn't know at the time was that although my fears were justified, I wasn't necessarily right about what or whom I should be afraid.

26
Bo and the Dildo

OVER THE NEXT few weeks Bruce and I spoke every night, often for an hour or more. Bruce was a great talker, and he reeled me in with romantic banter that I hadn't heard in a very long time, if ever. I was a sucker for kindness and an even bigger sucker for romance. Yet I noticed a subtle shift – there seemed to be a bit less urgency to his desire to actually see me. It was if our phone conversations were fulfilling his needs, that a voice on the phone was good enough for him. Two weeks of lengthy phone conversations went by before I realized that we still had no plans to see each other.

In the meantime, along came Bo. My friend Maureen had been dating a guy named Jimmy for several months. Jimmy was not one of my favorites but he seemed to make Maureen happy. And every time the three of us got together Jimmy found opportunities to tell stories about his "millionaire friend, Bo."

According to Jimmy, Bo had two homes, one in South Florida and another in Ohio about an hour away from me. He would soon be traveling back north for the summer and Jimmy insisted we meet. Despite some misgivings about where things did or didn't stand with Bruce, I wanted to say yes. I wasn't going to turn down dates (especially with a supposed millionaire) just because I'd met a guy who was fun to talk to on the phone. The little voice in my head said not to trust Bo, but I overruled it and agreed to meet him anyway.

As it happened, Heidi's Passion was co-sponsoring an all-male review at a local club that Saturday night and I'd committed to work a booth at the event. Maureen and Jimmy thought it would be fun to meet me there, and took it upon themselves to tell Bo about it. The next day Maureen called me to tell me that Bo was excited to meet me, and that the thought of seeing me working at a male strip review had "turned him on."

This wasn't just a red flag – it was a giant neon sign flashing "Danger, Horn-Dog approaching." I expressed my misgivings to Maureen, but she told me not to overthink it. Bo was a great guy, just wait.

The booths were in a large back room of the club. Heidi's Passion had one of the three "sponsorship" booths, each of which was geared to erotica of one form or another. (There was also a fourth booth, manned by a local chiropractor; I was afraid to ask what could possibly be so erotic about a back adjustment). The purpose of my booth was twofold – to sell products and to get women to book parties. I was having a lot of success with both, and by midnight, when the party started winding down, I was feeling pretty good. I'd spent the better part of four hours talking to women about love and sex, I'd been watching a bunch of hot male strippers out of the corner of my eye, and I'd booked ten parties.

Finally at midnight the party became co-ed, and husbands and boyfriends started filtering in. What I didn't know was that Maureen, Jimmy and Bo had been at the bar for over an hour, drinking and waiting to come in. At the stroke of midnight they were at my booth, watching as I was packing up my lubes and dildos.

Maureen was giggly-drunk. "Bo is soooo hot, you are in trouble, he couldn't keep his eyes off of you," she gurgled, as if Bo wasn't standing right there, which he was. I looked up at him and had to agree that he was pretty hot. He was just over six feet with a jutting, cleft chin, smoky eyes, and long black hair that flowed down and over his shoulders. He looked more like one of the dancers than a blind date.

Maureen was right about another thing; Bo exuded sex. I didn't see myself that way but he sure did. He had a smug smile on his face as he looked at me, surrounded by my lubes and dildos. It was the kind of smile that was big enough to let me know he was happy to see what he was seeing, but small enough to let me know that he, not I, was in control. This guy sure seemed to know what he was doing.

"Bo, this is Heidi," said Maureen, stating the obvious. Bo looked at me, and didn't say hello. I held out my hand to shake and say "Nice to meet you," but was embarrassed to realize my hand held a large vibrator. As I put it down, Bo, still not saying anything, came around behind the booth, wrapped one arm around my waist, drew me into him, and planted a big kiss on my lips. It was a very good kiss. But then he made his first misstep – instead of not saying anything, or letting his eyes doing the talking (and boy, could they talk), he said, "Hey Sugar, it's great to meet you. I've been enjoying you all night." This was just too cliché – and red flag #2.

We all were hungry and agreed to try to find a place to eat. We went to four restaurants but by this point it was nearly 1 AM, and none of them were serving food. Bo mentioned several times how this would not be a problem in South Beach, and that he could call his pilot and have us eating breakfast in Miami before dawn. Maureen and Jimmy seemed ready to say yes, and even I was tempted (I was child-free for the weekend), but something told me to say no thanks. Maybe it was because I wasn't as drunk as they were. Maybe it was the way that Bo's stories kept on reminding us about how much money he had. Or maybe it was the way he kept on calling me "Sugar," or "Shuug," which became less endearing with each repetition. But for whatever reason, I turned down the private jet. He seemed baffled and said, "Sure, another time." Then, "Hey Shuug, I'm a gourmet cook, let's go back to your place and I'll whip us up a meal." I was already wondering whether I'd made a mistake turning down South Beach, and I didn't want to say no twice. So the four of us headed to my house for a very late dinner.

Bo may have overstated his case a bit by claiming to be a gourmet chef, but he wasn't half bad, especially since he was forced to make do with the random items I'd picked up at the supermarket over the past few days. The pasta and salad he whipped up were pretty good and went so well with the wine I provided that thankfully nobody noticed what cheap wine it was. (Or, if they noticed they were too polite to mention it). Bo seemed to be in full seduction mode, showering me and my home with compliments at every opportunity. He must not have been as good at it as I thought he was, because it seemed so painfully obvious what he was doing. I was surprised to find myself thinking of Bruce. Here I was with this really hot, super-rich guy in my living room obviously trying to seduce me, and my thoughts were turning to a guy I talked to on the phone all the time but who seemed to have little interest in seeing me. What was up with that?

My Bruce vs. Bo trance was finally broken when, sometime between 3 and 4 A.M., Maureen and Jimmy announced they were ready to leave. Bo winked at them and me and said, "Hey Sugar, I can't drive home, I need to stay over at your place." He wasn't even pretending this was about anything besides getting laid. Suddenly the seduction didn't seem so seductive. I told him – in front of Maureen and Jimmy to make sure the point wasn't lost – that yes, he could sleep over, but it would be on the couch. No sex tonight, SUGAR!

He shrugged his shoulders and said, "It's cool, Shuug." We said goodnight to Maureen and Jimmy, who probably shouldn't have been driving, either, but I was too focused on my Bo problem to worry about their problem. They said their goodnights and headed out the door as I started gathering sheets, blanket and a pillow for Bo's night on the couch. Bo watched me as I tried to make the couch as comfortable-looking as I could. Then he said, "You're way too uptight, Shuug. The way you were playing with all of those dildos and dongs tonight, I thought you'd be all juiced up and an ANIMAL in the bedroom." Eeew. I told him he was right, I'm pretty uptight, and that the only animal in my bedroom is the dog. I wished him a pleasant good night and went into my bathroom to change into pajamas and brush my teeth. And I came out to find Bo standing stark naked in my bedroom. He looked me up and down, made a couple of the fuck-me moves I'd seen from the male dancers early in the evening, and started singing Marvin Gaye's "Let's Get It On."

He wasn't a very good dancer, and an even worse singer. Plus he didn't look nearly as hot naked as he had in his clothes. All I could think was, now what?

Thinking fast, I said the first thing that came to mind: "What the FUCK are you doing?" Eloquent, right? Even before he could answer, I noticed something odd about him, if there could be anything more odd than the fact that he was naked in my bedroom dancing and impersonating Marvin Gaye. What was odd was that from the neck down there wasn't a hair on his body. He looked like a shaved sheep. I couldn't help myself, I stared at his hairless balls, and asked, "What happened to all your hair?" As if this was the most natural question in the world, he calmly explained that he had a "waxer" come to his home every week. It seemed that he was about to start telling me more about his waxing habit, but my curiosity had already waned. I told him to get out of my room and get dressed before I called the police. The word "police" seemed to sober him up. He said, "Really?" and I said, "Really." With that he meekly left the room like a dog that had just been scolded for peeing on the floor. I didn't hear another word out of him, but I listened at the door until I was sure he was on the couch and he'd turned the lights out. And finally I got to sleep, making sure my bedroom door was securely locked. It was nearly 5 AM.

I woke up just a few hours later when my circadian alarm clock went off. My first thought was that my experiences with Bo had been a bad dream. My second thought was that my bad dream seemed to be snoring in the living room. I checked to make sure my bedroom door was still locked, and got into the shower, locking the bathroom door, too, just to be safe. I got dressed and went into the kitchen to make coffee, making as much noise as I possibly could. The snoring continued, unabated. Finally I took a more direct route, standing over him saying his name. Still nothing, so I shook his shoulders. Finally he sputtered awake, looking less like a GQ millionaire and more like a hung-over college kid who'd passed out the night before and didn't know where he was. "You need to get up and out of here," I said as abruptly as I could muster. Before he could answer I noticed his clothes in a pile on the floor, and I remembered his hairless body. "I'll let you get dressed," I said as I scurried back to my bedroom. I listened as he stirred around, and when I thought it was safe I came back out.

Thankfully he was dressed, and helping himself to the remainder of the coffee. His first words of the morning were, "I'm sorry about last night," to which I responded, "You should be, you were an asshole, even if you were pretty fucked up." He looked down and said, "Yeah, I guess you're right." Then a bit of the old Bo reappeared, "Too bad you didn't take me up on the trip to Miami, we would have had a lot more fun." As if the only problem with his behavior was that it was in my bedroom instead of Miami. "Yes, I'm sure we would have," I lied. He responded, "You're a really, fun, pretty, sexy woman. I hope I can see you again sometime?"

What could I say to that? What should I have said? In hindsight there were so many available responses more creative than what I did say, which was, "Maybe, we'll see." That's great, Heidi, you sure told him! He walked out the door and I watched as his rental car backed out the driveway and drove off. I got back into my pajamas and into bed. As I fell asleep, I thought about the moment I'd met Bo – I was working a male strip show, and holding a vibrator. And I was surprised that he thought I'd be easy to sleep with? Give me a break. That was it – never again would I allow a guy to see me with a vibrator in my hand on a first date. Men just couldn't be trusted with that kind of imagery.

27

The Blackout Means Free Publicity

IT WAS A warm August night and I had just returned home from a Heidi's Passion party when a huge storm hit. Thus began the Great Blackout. Much of the northeastern U.S. as well as big chunks of Canada lost power. What mattered to me was that Cleveland, and more specifically my house, also went dark. It had been a sultry day, in the high eighties, and nightfall didn't bring much cooling. There were rumors going around that the power could be off a long time and I was worried about losing the food in my freezer, so foolishly or otherwise, I pulled out all my frozen meat and fired up the grill. Fortunately I was a big user of candles – for everything from Jewish holidays to romantic mood lighting – so I had plenty of light. Although my cell phone service became spotty – apparently lots of overloaded circuits with everyone calling everyone else to talk about the blackout – my landline still worked. And to my delight, the first person to call was Bruce. He said he wanted to make sure I was okay.

I thought that was very sweet, and told him so. We chatted for a while. My libido was still engaged from the party earlier, so as soon as I learned he was child-free, I asked him if he wanted to come over. He said no thanks, he'd prefer to stay where he was until the power came back on. I wanted to ask why he preferred to stay home alone in the dark, but it seemed pointless. It was getting weird, a guy calls you every night, keeps telling you how wonderful he thinks you are, but has zero interest in seeing you? I told him my grill was ready so I needed to go. And I resolved to cut the cord with him. I appreciated his friendship but I couldn't accept someone who talked like we were more than friends but behaved otherwise. "Goodbye, Bruce," I said to the darkness of my backyard, lit only by the glowing coals of my grill and a couple of citronella candles.

The next day I was one of the few people in the neighborhood whose electricity had returned. I decided to play my own version of the Red Cross, delivering hot coffee to my family and friends and collecting freezer goods to store at my house. I had thrown on my Heidi's Passion shirt and a pair of tight jeans from the night before, which caused a bit of a stir in several of the houses. Most people in the neighborhood were okay with my side business but there were others who judged me both privately and publicly. Two people asked whether I was embarrassed to wear that T-shirt – clearly implying that I should be – and one told her son not to come downstairs while I was there. Another friend called her husband in to "see Heidi's shirt" He was practically drooling and she couldn't take her eyes off my breasts where the words Heidi's Passion was written. They wanted to know if I wanted to stick around and join them "for some fun." It took me a few minutes to understand what they were interested in, and when I did, I bolted. I began wondering how many of these people were truly my friends. Here I thought I was being a good neighbor and friend by bringing care packages to blacked-out homes, and all they're reacting to is the shirt I'm wearing, or what's underneath it? I was working hard to make money. Heidi's Passion was a legitimate business, and if it was such a bad thing, why were so many people coming to our parties and spending so much money on our products?

After several hours of visits and conversations and feeling judged and ogled by all these supposed "friends" I returned home. I needed to regroup. So I pulled out my CD player and meditation tapes and set up my lounge chair under a big tree in my front yard. But as so often happens, somehow my decision to meditate never turned into actual relaxation. I manage to utter just a single "OM" before I was interrupted by the sound of a truck. I looked up and saw a really cute guy leaning out the driver side window. He shouted out, "Hello, what's up with you?" and then asked, "Do you have power?"

It should have been pretty obvious I had power, since my house lights were on. My mind raced into fantasy mode. Here was Prince Charming, albeit in a white van instead of on a white horse. Then he asked me, "How were you affected by the blackout?" That seemed to be a pretty weird pick-up line, at least until I noticed the writing on the back of his van. It was a news truck. Now the other guy in the truck, who was even cuter than the driver, got out and asked me what I'd done before my power came back. I said I wished I could tell them I did something exciting or romantic, but that all I did was grill a bunch of frozen meat, and then, when my power had returned, made a couple of pots of coffee, delivered it to my friends who were still without power, and picked up a bunch of ice cream and frozen spinach to keep in my freezer. They both were gazing at me a little longer than normal, not quite enough to make me uncomfortable, though. They exchanged glances and the passenger, who turned out to be the reporter, asked if he could interview me. I thought back to my stint on the radio talk show and figured why not, it was time to graduate from radio to TV! So I said sure.

The guys wanted to do the interview in my house, and started getting some equipment out of their truck. Once inside they started setting up lights and the reporter took down some personal information; name, address, phone number. After an anxious run to the bathroom mirror to see how I looked, I became the face of the blackout that day, wearing the same tight "Heidi's Passion" T-shirt I'd worn during my food deliveries. Unfortunately, my stint on the evening news came while the blackout was still going on, so half the people who might otherwise have watched it, couldn't turn their TVs on. Still I got a couple of those "Was that really you?" and "Oh my god, I saw you on TV!" phone calls. And I can only guess what the free advertising for Heidi's Passion was worth.

I was also not above advertising for dates. When the filming was done I asked the reporter whether it was possible to post my phone number and advertise me as "smart, pretty, caring and *available*."

They laughed, and we agreed they should add, "Call if you're normal." They reminded me I'd already given them my phone number, and that they'd talk to their producer about it. After they left I started wondering whether they were actually taking me seriously, and whether I actually wanted them to do that. But apparently their producer nixed the idea so I never had to find out.

Still I did get one request for a date out of my TV appearance. The next day the driver/cameraman called to ask me out. I asked him if he was single, and he said not really, he was in a relationship but she didn't mind if he dated other women. I asked him his age and learned I had graduated high school the year he was born. I said I was flattered but told him he might want to ask his girlfriend whether she was really as okay with him dating other women, especially women who are old enough to be his mother. And that was that. Though like with the guy who had invaded my tent on the island, once I'd said no, I immediately wished I hadn't. The guys I was dating all seemed to have weird emotional or psychological issues, anyway, so why not get a hot twenty-two year old body to go along them?

28
Hooked

FOR REASONS I didn't understand, Bo kept calling me after he returned to Florida. He kept inviting me to come visit him, and I kept saying no. As a further enticement he e-mailed me numerous photos of his art collection. I don't know much about art but the message was clear – he was rich, rich, rich. He knew I was living paycheck to paycheck, but if he thought his money would attract me to him he was wrong. It would have been easy to let some crazy, strange, rich, man who waxes his body save me. But his constant reminders of how wealthy he was only served to remind me of how lacking he was in what I really wanted – civility, warmth, and romance.

Bruce seemed to have all three. Despite my earlier pledge to swear off him, I kept taking Bruce's calls. So our conversations continued, along with my efforts to get him to agree to see me. Those efforts were mostly unsuccessful, but one day he surprised me by accepting my invitation to be my date at a Bar Mitzvah that was coming up in three weeks. Bruce had always been skittish about making plans more than a few days in advance; he apparently didn't want to make a commitment in any form. I hoped that his willingness to make even this little commitment told me that maybe I'd finally gained entrance to his emotional fortress. He'd certainly gotten into mine.

Meanwhile I had an unexpected treat – Sam was in town. He joined a group of my friends and my mother for an impromptu party. Sam was his usual handsome and charming self. He had everything I could want in a guy, except for a home in the same time zone. Another plus was his comfort with my toy business. Actually it was more than just comfort. He loved that I was in the business, and proactively tried to come up with ways to help me out. One of those occasions occurred on our night out, when I mentioned that we were kicking around the idea of a line of products geared to gay men. He said he knew the perfect person for us to meet, and gave me the name and phone number of his hair stylist. He said he would arrange an introduction.

Sam was true to his word, and a few weeks later I was in Chicago, drinking coffee in a hotel lobby with Darryl. He was very good-looking, and very entertaining. Like me he had a second job, but instead of selling sex toys it was doing drag revues. He showed me a few photos of himself as Liza Minnelli, and I found myself wishing my legs were half as good as his. He was excited about our proposed new product line. He assured me that gay men would be completely comfortable buying toys in someone's home or apartment. He urged me to carry as diverse a line of products as possible. Leaning over, he winked at me and whispered conspiratorially, "I have friends that would enjoy sitting on a vibrating orange parking cone." I laughed and told him that I didn't see myself walking into parties with a supply of orange parking cones. Still, point taken. I made a note to look for products that had a parking cone shape – this could be fun! And thus was born our "Gay Treasure Trove," soon to be a successful market niche for Heidi's Passion. In a short time I had become an expert on things I never dreamed possible, and was having knowledgeable conversations about gay sex with people who were straight, gay, bi-, and who knows what else. I was freaking myself out daily, but in a very good way.

Shortly after my return from Chicago, I was getting ready to take my son out to dinner for a belated birthday celebration (mine, not his). Over the noise of the hair dryer I heard the phone ringing. It was Bruce, asking what I was doing that night. I told him I was going to dinner with my son and he asked if he could come along. I asked my son what he thought, and he said, "Of course, Mom. You know I told you he likes you, and I know you're going to marry him." Feeling both excited and anxious, I invited him to join us. He said he would pick us up in 30 minutes.

My hair and makeup had suddenly taken on new urgency. It seemed that no more than ten minutes had passed when the doorbell rang. Bruce was standing there with a bottle of champagne and a whisper in my ear that he wanted to make the night romantic, even if my son was there. My son had been craving male attention and Bruce gave it to him in droves. My son was hooked.

And so was I. In my mind I stood on a beach, looking out across the sea. The gale signs were up, telling me not to enter the water. But all I could see were the gently rolling waves, inviting me in. My relationship with Bruce was either going to be very, very good, or very, very, bad. Meanwhile I took a step toward the water, then another, then another.

29
Fix a Heart, Break a Heart

MY BIOLOGICAL FATHER, George, who for the time being had successfully fought off colon cancer, was taken to the hospital for emergency bypass surgery. He was overweight, diabetic, and the most frustrating man I'd ever known. He refused to follow any rules, regardless of whether they were for someone else's benefit or his own. The doctors made it clear that this would not be an easy surgery, telling us to expect the worst while praying for the best.

In the hours before surgery, as he lay in pre-op, I had a heart-to-heart with him, something we'd never had before. He looked rather pathetic in his gown, his hair unwashed and face unshaven. As we spoke I felt more like his mother than his daughter. I told him what I was really thinking, about how aggravating it was that he failed to take care of himself, and how upsetting it was to think that my brother and I might be burying him before his granddaughter made it to her Bat Mitzvah. I told him that I wanted him there, and that I expected him to fight to make that happen. He nodded and said that he would, although I couldn't read him well enough to know whether I'd really gotten through to him at all.

His surgery was scheduled for six the next morning. That night I felt as lonely and put-upon as I'd ever felt. My anxiety over George's health, my own finances, the children, and an upcoming court date with my ex over my claims for unpaid child support left me feeling like George was standing on my chest instead of lying in a hospital bed. I was desperate for companionship, but not the kind my children could give. I needed to be needy, and to find someone who would think that was OK. So I called Bruce, who promised to come over to my house with some TLC and a big joint for me to smoke.

Soon eight o'clock had come and gone. Then nine o'clock. By ten o'clock it was clear Bruce was a no-show. I called him at home and on his cell. He answered neither. I didn't leave messages. Instead I turned my phone off, and fell asleep on the couch, crying for what I might lose (George), for what I could lose (my house and kids), and for what I had apparently already lost (Bruce).

I woke early the next morning, anxious to get to the hospital so I could see my father before he went into surgery. On my way out the door, I turned my phone back on and saw I had two messages. The first was from Bruce, apologizing for not coming over, supposedly because "something came up" with his ex-wife and children. The second message was from a friend of mine, telling me she'd run into Bruce that night, at a restaurant where he and his ex-wife were having what appeared to be a romantic night out. She said she knew how I felt about Bruce, so she thought she should let me know what was going on.

On my way to the hospital I decided to do something for myself for a change. So I called Bruce, not caring how early it was or whether I woke him. He didn't answer, which was fine with me. I told him how disappointed I was in him, that I had misread him as a man who could be counted upon. I told him that I had no time for men who played games, lied, and made promises they were unable, unwilling, or just didn't care enough to keep. I told him we were done, and not to try calling me again. I hung up, feeling much better about myself. As painful as it was to have to give up the fantasy of my relationship with Bruce, it was liberating to be sticking up for myself for a change. By telling him I deserved better, I felt I was starting to believe it myself.

As the doctors had warned us, the surgery was a long one. I sat there all day until they finished in the early evening. Many visitors came in and out, so many that after a while I started wishing I could just be left alone. And wished that even more so when Bruce showed up. I wouldn't let him come up, so we talked in the hospital lobby.

I was adamant that I wanted no more intimacy with him, that I was done with him. But he begged and cajoled until I agreed, reluctantly, let him take me to lunch. We went next door to a coffee shop, and at first we didn't talk about us. Instead he expressed his empathy for what I was going through. He explained that the last time he'd been in a hospital, his mother had been dying and he talked openly about his experience. Bruce was his usual smooth self, and despite my best efforts I felt my anger and disappointment in him ebbing away. But I fought back, telling him bluntly that I no longer trusted him. He was screwed up, I said. He had commitment issues of some kind, plus some kind of weird goings-on with his ex-wife, not to mention that he'd completely let me down the night before at a time of great need. So as far as I was concerned, we were done. I told him he didn't need a girlfriend, he needed a therapist.

I wish I could say that was where this episode ended. That I told Bruce to go screw himself, that I didn't need his shit and that I strode back into the hospital, head held high, proud of what I'd done. Unfortunately my behavior has rarely gone according to script, and this day was no exception. When I told Bruce how screwed up I thought he was, Bruce admitted I was right. He added how impressed he was that I was willing to tell him that to his face, nobody else had ever talked to him so directly. This was what made me so special to him. He leaned forward, and spoke of how unique I was, how much I meant to him, how much he needed me. I told him I needed to get back to the hospital. We walked outside, he took my hand in his. He looked like he was almost in tears as he put his arms around me and hugged me. The hug felt too good for my own good. Soon we were kissing. He said he would call me, and that what had happened the previous night would never happen again.

When he left, I sulked back into the hospital. There was no glow from the kiss. There were no thoughts of how proud I was that I'd stood up for myself. Instead all I could do was wonder what the fuck was wrong with me.

30
Post-Op and In OP

MY FATHER PULLED through. But the recovery process was long and demanding, requiring much care from family members and his ex-wife. I took the early morning shift. On many days I had to set my alarm at 4 A.M. so I could wake, dress, make the twenty-minute drive to get to him by 5 A.M., then hurry home to get the kids off to school and be at one or the other of my dental hygiene jobs by 8. On a busy day I might then see as many as fifteen patients before finally getting home by 6 P.M., after which I still had to make dinner for the kids, help them with homework and get them to bed. And on Friday and Saturday nights I had my toy parties. Each night my main goal was to stay awake just long enough to get everything done before I collapsed into bed so I could start all over the next morning.

From Bruce's perspective this created an ideal scenario. We talked on the phone and he could offer encouraging words, but I was so busy that I had no time to see him. He claimed to be falling for me. He told me he'd never met anyone like me. I'm sure he was right. Where else might he have encountered a woman who had three jobs, was caring for and supporting her children with little or no support from their father, was paying for a Bat Mitzvah by selling dildos, and spending her weekends talking endlessly about sex while never having any of it herself?

I did manage to see Bruce on a few rare occasions, but the visits were few and far between. It was as if I wasn't allowed to see him until we'd racked up at least fifteen or twenty hours of phone time. And then we'd meet for coffee, or if I was really lucky, a glass of wine, after which I'd have to start running up the phone time in the hopes of getting to see him again a week or two later. Sad to say, even this "relationship" was a whole lot better than anything else I'd had since my divorce.

Still I was smart enough to know this wasn't what I was looking for, and I certainly wasn't going to take myself off the dating market. After all, I had 79 more dates to go. Then Bruce told me he was falling in love with me and that he could see us building our lives together. My head spun. I really wanted to believe in him.

But women I knew continued to send me warning flags up the pole. One of my patients told me she heard I was seeing Bruce. She said she knew him well, that he was a player who comes on fast and then runs away. Another told me that he had reeled in one of her friends with romantic words, and then broken her heart when he suddenly stopped calling for no reason. I listened and worried. I had every reason to believe them, and I think I actually did. But what if they were wrong? What if this time, Bruce really meant it? Was I prepared to walk away from even the small possibility of a life with him, just to protect myself from the risk of heartbreak?

Maybe I was being rational, or maybe (and more likely) I was just being fearful and insecure. But I decided to ignore his track record with me and these other women I was hearing about, and to take a chance with Bruce. If something bad came to pass, at least I would never have to wonder what might have been, like I kept wondering about all the twenty-year-old bodies I kept turning down. And besides I'd have no one to blame but myself, which was a situation that felt very familiar to me.

Meanwhile the dental office became the one place where I could relax and feel some semblance of security and contentment. Many of my patients had been coming to me for years and looked forward to the "dentaltainment" I offered them. I was like a combination of a stand-up oral comedian and dental shrink. Between the scraping and spitting, my patients shared their secrets with me, and I reciprocated like they were old trusted friends. This meant I gave and received a lot of unsolicited advice about life. Bruce was a hot topic, but since so many of my patients knew about Heidi's Passion, I got a lot of questions about sex.

One day I was doing a cleaning for a middle-aged female patient. When I briefly took my fingers and instruments out of her mouth, she said, "May ask a serious question?" I said sure. She asked, "Is oral sex bad for your teeth?" My answer: "Not if you floss after." The laughter from down the hall told me that our conversation had not been quite as confidential as she or I had thought.

Next thing I knew she was asking me to do a party for her, though having learned how easily sound travels in a dental office, she asked quietly. I agreed and booked the party; it was going to be in a few months, for her women's church group. I was looking forward to that one!

Not long after that, a seventy-year-old female patient told me she'd heard I was some kind of sex therapist, and asked whether I had any idea what she could do about her vaginal dryness. I told her I knew of many lubes that could help, and convinced her to have a party, too. After all, if she was dry, probably most of her friends were dry, too. She called me the next week to schedule it. She told me she'd lined up about sixty women. SIXTY women? Where had a seventy-year-old woman found sixty women to come to a sex toy party? I didn't ask. I had a Bat Mitzvah to pay for. Who was I to judge?

And so the hygienist's chair continued to be a great source of sex toy business for me. I sometimes wondered how many of my patients were using their teeth cleaning as an excuse to talk about sex. But I didn't care. If it was good for business, then keep it coming. And I began to think about which sex toys might be of interest to women old enough to remember when television couples like Dick Van Dyke and Mary Tyler Moore always slept in separate beds. God forbid someone should think they were actually having sex.

31
Happy Endings

MY DAUGHTER'S BAT Mitzvah day finally arrived. She did very well that morning and so did I. Well, maybe not quite so well. I had somehow deleted the speech I was supposed to give at the temple. So, that morning I found myself rewriting the entire speech when I should have been getting dressed and doing my makeup. I was so stressed out that I dropped my daughter off at the wrong hair salon. I had to go back and pick her up, take her to the right one, and we were thirty minutes late getting there. As you can imagine, soon she was as stressed as I was. But like me, she managed to collect herself and perform beautifully in the ceremony. It was one of the most exciting days of my life.

I never wanted my kids to feel like they were any different from any of their friends. And rightly or wrongly, most of the kids were more focused on the parties than the ceremonies. As such, I considered it of the utmost importance for me to give my daughter a party, regardless of my finances.

I came up with an option that provided a reasonable ratio of fun-to-cost. Our party that night was at a farm southeast of the city. We had planned hayrides and bonfires, but those went awry when the weather turned up cold and rainy, and the hay proved infested with red ants. We had three dozen thirteen-year-old girls shrieking in unison. This was not exactly how we'd planned it. So the hayride was postponed while fresh hay was brought in, although when it resumed about half the girls declined to participate.

Bruce was there, too, and did everything right. He was warm, engaging, and acted perfectly the part of Mom's boyfriend. Late in the evening, as the girls were off dancing and giggling with the few boys my daughter had invited, Bruce found me in a corner of the tent. He took my hands in his, and told me he loved me. He said he thought I was the greatest woman he'd ever met and that we could make each other's worlds so much better together than they'd been apart. Every word, phrase and line was perfect. Just as my daughter was able to overlook the rain and red ants to go to sleep that night satisfied and content, I was able to ignore all the *mishegas* in my life and focus on the present – a present in which I was very, very happy.

My parents had given me a trip for two to Las Vegas for my 40th birthday. I had purposely planned it for a few weeks after the Bat Mitzvah, and naturally, I invited Bruce. I'd assumed he'd say yes and eagerly anticipated my first time traveling with a boyfriend, and my first visit to Vegas. Unfortunately, Bruce's enthusiasm did not match mine, and when I invited him he flatly turned me down. I all but begged him to come with me, but he refused. He said he "had too many things to do at home," though he never explained exactly what those things were. Once again the closeness I felt from him was misleading. It was a push-me/pull-me situation that I wanted to run from but felt powerless to escape. I felt rejected and confused. My friends showed endless patience in listening to my broken record complaints about Bruce but it was starting to get old for them and for me. They didn't understand the hold Bruce had on me, and when they asked me to explain it, I couldn't.

My friend Nancy finally said to me, "Enough is enough. If that asshole doesn't want you, then stop wasting your time. Take _me_ to Vegas, we'll have a blast." Nancy was recently-divorced and a bit of a wild child. I suspected that her idea of a "blast" would probably be pretty memorable.

So I took Nancy to Las Vegas. I told Bruce how upset I was that he wasn't there, and he responded by calling me twice a day to tell me how much he missed me and that he couldn't wait to take me to Las Vegas with him the next spring. He also promised me a weekend away with him, something he'd been promising for a long time, but still hadn't delivered on. He kept saying the right things. He said we needed to spend some time alone, and again I talked myself into believing him.

In the meantime I had arrived in Las Vegas with Nancy and I decided to make the most of it. Nancy's divorce had been grinding on, so she was equally motivated to cut loose. We ate, drank, gambled as much as our meager finances would allow, and flirted shamelessly with every man in sight. We both had our mojos going. I won a $1000 jackpot on a slot machine, which I think was the first time I'd won anything in my life. I decided to splurge, and booked us a day at the hotel spa. We arrived early, put on our robes, and sipped green tea as we waited for our services. I was up first for a massage. My masseur came out and introduced himself as Stavos. I asked him where the name Stavos came from, and he told me he was Greek. By the way, he was absolutely gorgeous. Nancy winked and said, "Don't do anything I wouldn't do." Knowing Nancy, that didn't exclude much.

Stavos led me into the room. Sitar music was playing amidst candlelight, as I smelled aromas of jasmine, vanilla, and who knows what else. It was meant to be relaxing, but instead the combination of candlelight, music, aromas, and a Greek god of a masseur made it feel like the most romantic date I'd ever been on, times twelve. I lay face down on the massage table, the Egyptian cotton sheets brushing softly and sensually over my back. Stavos pulled back the top of the sheet, put warm oil on his hands and started working on my neck and shoulders. Within five minutes I was about as horny as a woman could possibly be. I was glad I didn't have a penis, because my erection would have been quite impossible to hide. Instead, I tried to calm myself down by meditating, but it was challenging with Stavos' hands all over me. I started drifting off in a haze of pure ecstasy. He was rubbing my backside and my inner thighs in mesmerizing circular motions, and without even realizing it, I let out a deep moan. This only made his hands linger more on my behind and inner thighs. I was in a spell, and happy to be there.

He told me to turn over. I rolled onto my back. He placed a warm scented towel over my eyes and whispered into my ear. "Are you doing all right?" The warmth of his breath and the sound of his sexy voice in my ear sent shivers down my spine. He applied more hot oil to his hands and started working on my quads. His hands gently brushed under the area covered by the towel. I didn't think I could take any more and decided to throw caution to the wind. I let another moan escape my throat, and I opened my legs a little wider.

Stavos knew exactly what he was doing. I opened wider. Eventually his hands went all the way, and so did I. I could only hope that the sitar music had been loud enough to mask the sounds of my orgasm. Needless to say, he earned a VERY big tip that day.

When it was all over, I went to look for Nancy. She took one look at me and said, "Oh my God, look at your face! What happened in there?" "Women can get happy endings too," I said, winking. Nancy gave me a stunned look, and told me how jealous she was, which made it even better. Winning a thousand dollars and using a chunk of it to pay a gorgeous Greek hunk to give me an orgasm? No wonder people love Vegas!

32

Return to Reality, or Escape from Reality?

IT WASN'T EASY coming off the Bat Mitzvah and Vegas high. Slowly, I began to settle back into a routine with the kids, the house, my jobs, and Bruce. He and I had a few great nights together. He was no Stavos when it came to sex, though he was a good conversationalist. I didn't think it was possible to fall any harder for Bruce, but I did.

Then, out of the blue, he dropped yet another heartbreaking bombshell. Three Saturday nights in a row he told me he was unavailable because he was with his kids *and* their mom. I would never complain about his spending time with his kids, but his ex-wife was another matter. I finally told him I wasn't going to put up with that any more. He could date me or his ex-wife, but not both. Bruce responded by telling me how "confused" he was. He liked me, he loved me, he felt comfortable with me. He knew how good we were for each other. Yet when his ex-wife asked to get together (at least he claimed it was her making the advances, though I didn't know whether to believe him), he had a hard time saying no. I told him he needed to decide whether he was really divorced. And for the umpteenth time I resolved to stay away from him.

Just as he'd done every other time, the more I tried to pull away from Bruce, the harder he worked to reel me back in. He kept calling me, and the empathetic friend/therapist in me kept me answering and talking to him. Bruce seemed to be sinking into a depression, which was the last thing I needed in my life. It seemed that every time I started feeling good about myself and my life, I'd get a depressed call from him, which in turn reminded me of my inability to forge a relationship with him. I constantly found myself pondering what was I lacking that I couldn't convince him to give up his ex-wife? What was wrong with me, that he didn't want to see me or commit to me? His sadness was infectious and I needed to inoculate myself.

The vaccine, even if it was just a temporary one, came in the form of Doug. Doug was a friend of mine in high school and I'd run into him one night at a restaurant when I was out with my mom. He asked me out for coffee and I accepted. Over a couple of cappuccinos he confessed that he'd had a longtime crush on me. I decided that I couldn't – and didn't want to – resist. I accepted his invitation for another date, assuming (and hoping) that it would lead straight to the bedroom.

This was all so foreign to me. I had never felt so sexually carefree before. I'm not sure whether it was the parties, or my feelings of inadequacy with Bruce, or maybe Stavos that had led me there, but at the time, I didn't really care. Doug and I started hanging out together. Compared to Bruce, he was so easy to be with. No long, heavy discussions, no aura of depression. And most important, no ex-wife – he'd never been married and had no children. I didn't have the sense that this was going anywhere, as Doug didn't seem to have much interest in giving up his bachelorhood. But that just made it easier for me. For once I could just have fun, both socially and in the bedroom, without constantly worrying what it all *meant*. What a relief! Yet I still had my moments when I found myself wondering, what the hell am I doing?

As if to accentuate the point, Bruce learned that I was dating someone and started a full-court press. He called constantly, and I was forced to listen as his melancholy moods deepened. Sometimes I played social worker, stopping at his house on my way home from work or in-between carpooling to share a glass of wine, bring him food or to just hug him when he said he needed a hug. I didn't want to feel for him but I couldn't help it. He kept recounting, like some mantra, that things would work out for us, and that the pieces would fall into place if I would just be patient.

Bruce told me I was the one bright spot in his life. He said my visits helped him get through many days. I chose to believe him and tried to suppress my disappointment that what I'd thought could be a relationship between two lovers, had devolved into one between a patient and his therapist. Which left me where, exactly? I was having sex with Doug, with whom I had no emotional intimacy, while I was getting zero physical intimacy from a guy I'd really connected with emotionally. It reminded me of the complaints I used to get from my friends who play golf – some days they were great off the tee but couldn't putt, other days they could putt but kept slicing their drives. They couldn't seem to put it all together at the same time, and I wondered whether I would ever find an emotional connection and good sex in the same man. The odds of winning another jackpot in Vegas began to seem better than the odds of success in my search for a man.

33
You Go, Girls!

I HAD TO refocus yet again. Doug was eventually gone, and Bruce continued to suck me dry emotionally. I put my energies back into my family and work. I was slowly paying off the Bat Mitzvah bills with what I began to call my "Dildo Money." I continued to try to live my tripartite life of hygienist by day, dildo girl by night, and suburban single mom to boot. I decided that with all that, I simply didn't have time for men.

My party with my elderly patient and her sixty friends was coming up. I was really looking forward to it, as I enjoyed imagining that at age seventy, sex could still be a source of pleasure. Maybe there was hope for me after all?

The old ladies' party was an hour away from my home. On my arrival, I discovered the sixty attendees were mostly wealthy, and not all that old – there were plenty of twenty-somethings there to complement the eighty-year olds. It turned out that many of them were from the same family, including various cousins, sisters, aunts, and, of course, grandma. It was as if someone had called for a family reunion, but then the women sent all the men away so they could have a sex toy party. My kind of family!

One of the older women at the party was particularly inquisitive, asking questions about nearly every product I introduced. She also happened to be hard-of-hearing, so she didn't just ask the questions, she yelled them, and she kept making me repeat my answers, even when I tried yelling them back. Finally her younger sister, who may have been in her late sixties, began to translate my answers. So I would say, "This toy is for clitoral stimulation," and my translator would yell into her sister's ear, "This toy is for clitoral stimulation!" Or I would say, "You put this toy on the penis before intercourse and it will delay ejaculation," and she would shout, "You put this toy on the penis before intercourse and it will delay ejaculation!" I felt as if I were in a sexual echo chamber.

I eventually became accustomed to the echo, and even began to appreciate the extra emphasis the younger sister was giving my words. When I began to talk about some of our waterproof toys, however, the older sister turned to the younger one and yelled, "I use my finger in the bathtub to orgasm!" All conversation in the room stopped. Everyone exchanged glances and then all eyes then turned to me awaiting a response. But when I tried to talk, I just burst out laughing instead. Soon the rest of the room was doing the same. Meanwhile, I used the bathtub confession as a transition into the "Flower," a little pink waterproof vibrator that a woman of any age could use in the tub to achieve better orgasms than her finger could provide. After my translator yelled the description into her sister's ear, the 80-year-old turned to the front of the room and shouted, "Sold! It's time to give my finger a rest, I'm getting arthritis anyway!" She ended up spending over $150 on various toys – including the Flower – though it wasn't clear how much of it was for her and how much was for her sister. Either way she proved a great salesperson for me; I sold more Flowers that night than I usually sold in a month of parties combined.

I had never envisioned that a woman over 65 would have any interest in oral sex. Wrong! When I even mentioned oral sex techniques, a tittering went up around the room and I could see that nearly everyone was interested. Getting and giving seemed to be of equal interest to all the women. I imagined some of these women going back to their senior living communities or wherever they lived, and being very, very popular. Though to be honest, I had to stay in the moment, as the thought of my own parents, or worse yet grandparents, engaging in oral sex was less than attractive. Still, everyone is entitled to pleasure, no need to turn off your libido just because you need a walker to get around, right? I decided to suggest to my partner Heidi that we start to offer a senior-citizen discount. I was pretty sure we'd be the first one in the industry to do that.

The parties kept coming. The next night I had what I'd come to call an "average" party – maybe a couple of dozen women ranging from their 30s to late 40s. Though, even the average parties usually presented at least one memorable moment. Just like my dates. (I think I was up to #49 by then, and unfortunately I could still count on my fingers with a few left over, how many of the forty-nine guys had made it to a second date). That night, a woman asked if she could take my sample vibrator into the bathroom and try it before deciding whether to buy it. Believe it or not, I'd had this request before. A department store won't let you try on underwear before you buy it, why should you expect to be able to stick a vibrator in your vagina before you buy it? I gave her my usual response, which was "Trust me, you don't want to stick this inside you. I use it as a sample and thousands of hands have touched it." She answered with a straight face, "No problem, I'll put a condom on it. It'll still be cleaner than most of the dicks I've had." A shouting match ensued between her and some of her fellow partygoers; half of them accused her of being "a pig," the other half agreed with her and wanted her to go use the vibrator. I decided to move on to the anal beads, and prayed nobody would ask to try them out.

The more parties I did, the clearer it became that the younger the crowd, the less they spent. Maybe they didn't have the cash, or maybe their libidos were high enough that they didn't feel they needed as much help from sex toys. But the consistent pattern was that my highest grossing parties were with women in their late 30s and up. Some of them were, like me, single and interested in enhancing their ability to pleasure themselves. Others were in relationships and looking for ways to liven things up. In some cases, sadly, they were hoping to resurrect a sex life that had died on the vine. But regardless, I genuinely felt I was helping these people. It was as if

I were a Pied Piper of pleasure, leading my charges to a happier, healthier sex life. Sometimes I would lie in my bed and think about how many people, both men and women, were at that moment enjoying great sex thanks to a product I had sold them or advice I had given them. It was a great feeling, and helped soften the disappointment I felt over my own nearly nonexistent love life. I tried to reassure myself that someday sexual karma would kick in, and all this intimacy I was helping create for others would circle back to me. Meanwhile I went to bed alone, waiting for it to happen. And waiting, and waiting, and waiting.

34
Stocking Suffers

THE HOLIDAY SEASON was upon us and the party business was booming. I was doing two to three parties nearly every weekend. Apparently women all over Northeast Ohio were deciding that dildos made great stocking stuffers. I sold to younger women and older women, single women and married women, experienced toy users and those to whom even a little bottle of flavored lube seemed new and scandalous. It was a whirlwind of edutainment; I amused my audiences with jokes and stories as I taught them how to find their G-spots and sold them toys. It was a far cry from my periodontal probing of my patients' molars.

Our product line was growing as rapidly my customers' husbands' penises. We now had a slick, glossy catalogue that I distributed at all our parties. Our website was up and running and filled with a wide variety of toys that went well beyond what I was able to carry to the parties. For the parties, I had a large sample kit and got pretty good at keeping up with our many new items, although I made no further effort to try them all out, as I was afraid I might seriously injure myself if I did. Around the office my reputation as a sexpert far exceeded the actual sex I was getting, which was pretty much none. Nevertheless each day I brought in a new sex tip that I'd either taught or learned at one of my parties.

One day, my boss, right after admitting that he felt rather intimidated by the range of my sexual expertise, asked if I'd be willing to do a couples' holiday toy party for his co-ed softball team. I wasn't sure how I felt about talking about Pocket Rockets and coochie cream in front of my boss, but by this point I'd done it in front of so many people that I had become all but immune to any possible embarrassment. Still, I didn't say yes until I'd extracted a promise that he would give me a week off between the holidays.

The party took place in a large, beautiful old home in what passes for the "country" in the Cleveland suburbs. When I arrived, I wasn't sure whether this was really a sex toy party or just a holiday get-together, as the house was decorated to the hilt for Christmas. It was draped with evergreen branches, laurels, pinecones, and "happy holidays" banners all over the place. There was a fifteen-foot Christmas tree in the entry with presents strewn underneath; I couldn't help wondering whether after our party, there would be some new (and much more fun) packages under the tree. The food was abundant, and the drinks had already been flowing for several hours by the time I arrived. The hostess directed me to the great room, where chairs had been set up and a makeshift "stage" had been created in front. I set up a folding table and began laying out my samples, as well some products designed to appeal to couples, plus a large selection of pornographic movies.

I sensed someone standing behind me and turned around. A middle-aged man, a bit round in the belly and bald on the top, stood before me. Apparently wanting to skip any pleasantries, he didn't even say hello. Instead he asked me directly whether it was true that I was available? I smiled at him (he was, after all, a potential customer), and said, "Are you asking if I'm single?" He said, "No, I mean 'available' as in, do you think you'd be willing to come home with my wife and me tonight?" I assumed this was not an invitation to come over for a cup of coffee. After thanking him for the offer, I politely declined, using the somewhat truthful excuse that I preferred not to mix business with pleasure. Seeming genuinely disappointed and not the least bit embarrassed, he said he'd let his wife know, and returned to the party. I decided I would not even try to figure out which woman was his wife; if she started asking questions about toys during the party, I didn't want to be distracted (or grossed out) at the thought that she was imagining using them on me.

That was just the first of three offers I got that night to participate in a threesome. In each case the offer was made by the man, leaving me to wonder whether the wives were really as interested as the husbands were saying they were. But it was easy to say no. I didn't have that much interest in a threesome, and if I were to try one, it certainly wasn't going to be with someone who was close enough with my boss to be invited to his Christmas party.

With all the threesome proposals that were going around, it was almost a relief when another guy who I thought was hitting on me turned out just to be trying to fix me up on a date with a friend of his. He proved to be a bit on the aggressive side, however. Immediately after he finished telling me about his single friend, and before I could respond, he took out his cell phone and dialed his friend. "Hey dude, come over to Bill's, he's got the team here for a sex party and the sex toy lady is hot and single." I had no desire to hear where the conversation was going from there, so I scurried away to tell the hostess it was time to start the party.

She gathered everyone into the room. I estimated there were about three dozen people there, at least a third of whom, it seemed, had already propositioned me. I launched into my sales pitch, starting with some of the more tame romance items, like bubble bath powders and bath candles. That led to scented massage oils, which led to erotic massages. The women seemed mostly nonplussed, but some of the men, who seemed pretty well-lubricated (with alcohol, not the other kind) started asking "Heidi" questions.

"Do *you* like that?" "Have you actually used all those things?" "How many orgasms have you had?" "Do you make a lot of noise?"

Several of the men soon stopped even pretending to pay attention to the toys and focused entirely on me. Finally, my boss stood up and told everyone to stop acting like hormonal teenagers and to let me do my thing. The guys quieted down, but I was pissed. So I thanked my boss for the support and added, "For the record, for those of you acting tastelessly and asking me inappropriate questions, I will say this once and clearly so there are no mistakes. I will not today, or ever, have sex with any of you, with or without your wives. My own sex life is irrelevant to this party. If you want me to continue I will, but if you can't or won't behave yourselves, I will pack up and come back when it's just the women."

There was a long moment of silence, until the hostess finally said: "All right boys, that's about enough. Let's all have some fun and Heidi is off-limits for anything but advice." To my relief, the men actually behaved after that. They even asked questions that were focused more on romance than on the orgasm angle. They ended up buying lots of massage stuff – the drunker they got, the more they spent. Chalk one up for the guys. Meanwhile, the women bought lingerie and toys. There was going to be a lot of good sex going on that night, assuming the men weren't too drunk to participate. And my irritation over how the evening had begun was cured by the wads of cash in my purse.

That party proved to be the perfect kick-off for a very profitable holiday season. Between word-of-mouth advertising and my ever-improving sales skills, the average profitability of my parties was way up. It wasn't uncommon for me to net five hundred dollars or more in cash at a single party, and I was doing two, sometimes three parties a week. On top of finally being able to pay all our bills and school expenses, I was also making a dent in the debt that I had accumulated after my ex lost his job and stopped sending checks. I had wanted more than anything to be able to keep my kids living in our new home and in the schools they were already in, and for the first time it seemed I might be able to pull it off. Even better, I wasn't doing anything illegal or even (in my book) immoral to get there. I was truly at peace with my dildos.

35
The Robbery

OUR SAMPLE LINE was up to about 1500 items. Even as the product lines grew, I continued my practice of carrying them in suitcases from party to party, seeing as how I couldn't come up with a better method. This posed a bit of a problem when my kids and I prepared for our annual trip to visit my parents in Florida, because we needed the suitcases for our clothes. So I did what any mother engaged in a frenzied last-minute packing spree would have done. I took the samples out and threw them into my bedroom. I stuffed some of them into my dresser drawers, and threw some of the bigger items into my closet. Under my bed I crammed a wealth of vibrators, lubes, books, and porn movies. I left my stacks of order forms and catalogs out on the floor in boxes.

As we sat at the airport waiting to board our plane, I was thinking how wonderful my parents were and how lucky I was to have them. They had sent us tickets to spend Christmas vacation with them and the rest of our relatives who lived down there. They knew how tough the past year had been on my children, and had insisted on giving us a gift of some time away. As we got on the plane and settled into our seats, the reading materials I stuffed into the seatback pocket reminded me of the mess I'd left in my bedroom. I resolved to devise a better inventory warehousing system after the first of the year.

Little did I know that this thought had come to me about one day too late.

My parents met us at the Fort Lauderdale airport. The kids were excited to swim and hang out with their grandparents and cousins. I was excited to do as little as possible. I wanted to sit at the pool and think about anything other than dental plaque, sex, money, dating, and Bruce. Bruce seemed to come and go like a menstrual cycle. Lately the frequency of his calls had been on the upswing, but his mood was on a downswing. His sadness had worsened and he was getting (or so he claimed) professional help. And depending on my own mood, I either felt repelled by his neediness and sought to avoid him, or felt seduced by his neediness and longed to be there for him. So I turned off my cell phone and headed to the pool. No patients, toy customers or depressed men, needy or otherwise, would be able to reach me.

And as far as I could tell, nothing bad had happened when I'd tuned out. What a relief! So I did it again the next day. But my luck didn't hold. I'd been at the pool maybe an hour on that second day before my mother came out and told me my brother, who'd stayed home in Cleveland, urgently needed to talk to me. My mother told me something had happened with my house and I should call him right away. As I dialed the phone I imagined a frozen water pipe, or maybe a broken furnace.

The truth was much worse. My brother's first words were, "I have some bad news. Someone broke into your house and ransacked it. What the fuck is in your bedroom? It looks like a bomb went off in a porno shop." A wave of nausea came over me. I felt myself beginning to hyperventilate as my brother went on. "There are two cops here and they both say they know you. One says he went to high school with you and the other says you clean his teeth. They want to know when you turned into a freak with all the sex stuff?"

I couldn't believe it. My house had been broken into, I had no idea what, if anything, had been stolen, and instead of talking about my TV or jewelry, all my brother — or apparently, the police — wanted to know about was why I had boxes of dildos in my bedroom. I was angry, but I tried to hide it from my brother, just as I'd hidden my sex toy business from him all along. When he'd first seen all the toys, he'd thought I was a hooker. I reassured him I wasn't and begged him to give me the details of the robbery. To shut him up, I promised a sex toy seminar when I got home, but all I cared about at that point was what had been taken by the burglars. Unfortunately, the answer was pretty much everything. TV, stereo, computers, all my jewelry, even my microwave and toaster oven, a nice set of kitchen knives and my grandmother's china were all gone. The burglars must have just pulled a moving van into the driveway and carried everything out.

    I couldn't even begin to image what it would cost to replace all this stuff. I had insurance, but how could I prove the value of what I'd lost, or even remember everything I had? When my brother heard me sobbing on the phone his attitude changed and his focus was finally redirected. He assured me he'd deal with the police and get my house cleaned up for me, so I could get some semblance of enjoyment out of the rest of my trip, if that was possible, which it wasn't. He also said that he was installing an alarm, better late than never.

    My ex heard about the robbery and he called me and told me the robbery was my fault. If he were still around he would have prevented this, and if we hadn't been divorced this wouldn't have happened. I told him to go screw himself, that I'd rather be robbed than married to him any day and hung up on him. Then Bruce called. How was everyone hearing about this? Apparently word was spreading like wildfire. I couldn't help but wonder whether word was also spreading about the contents of my bedroom. Bruce was at his supportive best. He said he would do whatever I needed to have done, and would pay for it all. I'd been there for him, he said, and now he wanted to be there for me. And as if he felt he was on a roll, he asked me if I was free on New Year's Eve, and if so did I want to go on a "very special date" with him. I wanted to say "no" and I wanted to say "yes." And you can guess by this point that "yes" won. My first day back from Florida, I went to the police station to file the official report. I had done the best I could to compile a list of everything they'd taken. It included a bunch of stuff from my sample kit, though for some reason, while they took the books, tapes, oils and lingerie, they left the vibrators and dildos behind. I was very nervous that the robbers would think I was some kind of sex machine and come back to see me in person. And it didn't help much when the female desk sergeant, upon learning who I was, said, "Oh Heidi, I heard about some of the fun stuff those burglars found at your house, and I think several detectives want to date... I mean talk to you."

The only thing that kept me from crying was that she asked for my card so she could book a party once I refilled my inventory. And the one consolation as the detectives intensively questioned me, was that I knew my unique case would not soon be forgotten. I also suspected that for the foreseeable future they'd be watching my house pretty closely. Thankfully, neither of them asked me out on a date, and I wondered what they'd say if I told them their desk sergeant was planning to host one of my parties. But her secret was safe with me, even if my own secrets apparently were not safe with anyone else.

36
Too Many Issues

BRUCE MOVED INTO my house for my first week back, while we waited for the alarm and new doors to be installed. (The burglars had entered by basically just kicking in the back door, so we decided to replace all the doors with something a little sturdier). It felt strange to have a man in the house, though "strange" in this case also meant comforting. I felt as if I were playing house, having a real, live man around. I liked it.

It felt like we were a real couple, doing things real couples do. We weren't just living together but were even going out together on New Year's Eve. Usually, I dislike going out to dinner on New Year's Eve – the restaurants are crowded, understaffed and overpriced. But that night everything seemed to work. We had a romantic dinner, made more so by his telling me he thought I was his soul mate and that we were meant to be together. As per usual, I was finding it increasingly difficult to keep my guard up.

Finally, the week ended. The alarm was set up and my new doors had been installed. Bruce moved out, and he immediately went back to his old self. We were back to talking hours a day and seeing each other only sporadically. I was baffled, distraught, and leaning hard on my friends. Somehow, I managed to keep forgetting Bruce's mood swings and his weird on-again, off-again relationship with his ex-wife. Instead, I reverted to wondering whether there was something wrong with me, that in some way I wasn't good enough for him. My self-esteem was dwindling and my friends were justifiably getting tired of hearing about it.

My party schedule was also a bit slow. This was a mixed blessing. It meant less income, but it also meant I had some time to get my children and my house put back together. I was busy trying to replace the stuff the burglars had stolen. It seemed that every day I noticed some other random thing I was missing. I also kept discovering hidden messes – a cord torn out of the wall here, or fingerprint dust the police had left on a countertop. I'd have felt better about the fingerprint dust if it had actually led to identifying a suspect. But the weeks went by and the police had no leads. I was still pretty freaked out thinking the robbers now would think of me as some kind of lusty sex kitten. I realized I'd reached a new low when I started worrying about what the burglars thought of me.

Bruce was still around, partly for better but mostly for worse. He cycled through a seemingly endless variety of highs and lows, sometimes on a daily or even hourly basis, and the lows seemed to be getting lower. I felt like I was in love with him, but in retrospect, given his antics, I can no longer remember why. Maybe it was just the mother in me. In between putting in my 40+ hours at the dentists' offices and trying to take care of my own two kids, I was caring for Bruce as if he were my third child.

I finally confronted Bruce (for the third or fifth or ten time) and told him I'd had it. But this time instead of swearing him off, I tried to spur him to action with an offer of my help. I told him he couldn't continue on the road he was on. For my sake, his sake, and both of our children's sake, he needed to do something. Anything. He agreed and admitted he had a problem. Unfortunately, the solution he proposed wasn't what I'd had in mind. I was hoping he would seek professional counseling (which he had previously claimed to be doing). Instead his solution was that he "just needed to get away."

The next morning he called me from the airport, just before he boarded a flight to some friend's house in a remote part of Mexico. He said was going to stay there for a month to clear his head. I was flabbergasted, realizing that I really had no clue whatsoever what was going on in his head. Saying goodbye to him should have been painful for me, but at that point I felt so numb that the pain barely registered.

Several days day after Bruce left, he called me from whatever remote Mexican village he'd run off to. He cried, said he wanted me to be with him, that he couldn't be alone. He asked whether I could take a long weekend and fly down. I told him I couldn't afford the plane fare, much less the lost income. We ended the conversation on a sad note. I wished him well and told him to call anytime he needed me, though as soon as the words came out, I wished I could take them back.

37
Putting the Oxygen Mask On

AFTER MY DIVORCE had been finalized, the legal and financial issues I faced after proved to be even harder than the divorce had been. By the time I had the balls to get out, I just wanted it to end. If I'd had a crystal ball, or the luxury of taking the time to consider everything, I would have addressed some of the financial issues and custody issues before the final papers were signed. But as hard as it was on me logistically and financially, it was worse knowing that my children were also feeling pain. My daughter had been seeing a child psychologist for a few years. My daughter was very bright but had recently been diagnosed with ADHD. After many visits, we finally agreed to try medication. The medication did wonders for her. At age thirteen it seemed we finally had her back on track.

Unfortunately, it wasn't quite as easy getting a clear-cut plan for my son. He was having a much harder time with the divorce. He was craving male attention, and also experiencing focusing and anxiety issues. We tried both conventional and unconventional approaches. He was seeing a psychologist, a neurologist, a biofeedback specialist, and his pediatrician. With the help of this team we felt we were making progress. But that progress was the result of regular visits as well as medication, all of which cost money. Money I didn't have, and money my ex sure as hell wasn't providing. The bills from all the treatments and medications for the kids were rapidly accumulating. I tried my best to keep up but kept falling behind. Eventually my son's team told me they couldn't keep treating him until I paid my bills.

Not knowing where else to turn, I visited a social services agency and asked for help. The social worker gave me an intake questionnaire to fill out. The questionnaire was an eye-opener. I'd thought I was at least aware of the issues in my life and that I'd already overcome a fair number of them. But my questionnaire responses told a different story. The questionnaire asked:

In the past year, have you:

(a) Been divorced?
(b) Had illness in you or a close family member?
(c) Had financial struggles?
(d) Moved?
(e) Had to deal with death?
(f) Had anyone in your life that is an addict?
(g) Been robbed or raped?
(h) Had job changes affect you?
(i) Been involved in any legal issues?
(j) Had stress in your life that has caused you illness or hospitalization?
(k) Had to care for someone that is ill?
(l) Do you feel stressed, on edge and have trouble sleeping?
(m) Is your temper uncontrollably short?

As I sat there answering "yes" to almost every question, I suddenly felt like my life was completely out of control. My vision of myself as a Supermom, taking on and overcoming each day's challenges, began to crumble. By itself, each challenge I faced had felt surmountable. But when confronted with this checklist of everything that was wrong with my life, doubt and panic crept in. I'd survived up to this point, but how could I get through another week, or month, or year of this? Much less the ten or fifteen years I would need to get the kids safely through college?

The social worker looked at my questionnaire responses and then back at me. "When you're on an airplane," she said, "why do you think they tell you to put the oxygen mask on yourself before giving it to your kids?" The answer was obvious. If I didn't take care of myself, I wasn't going to be able to take care of anyone else. She gave me the name of a group therapy program that my insurance would cover completely.

I'd like to say that I walked out of her office a changed woman, and that from that day forward I charted a new and healthier course for myself. But I didn't. Instead I did something really stupid. I called Bruce in Mexico. I told myself I was calling just to see how he was doing, but mainly I wanted to share with him how excited I was about what the social worker had told me. I thought that maybe I could encourage him to seek similar help.

He listened to everything I said. Then he begged me again to come down to Mexico to spend a long weekend with him. I again reiterated that I couldn't afford it. He told me he was so desperate to see me and that he would cover everything. Not just the plane fare, but any income I lost from not working the weekend. He said he would even pay any bills that came in during the week, if that was what it took to get me there.

Seduced by a man so desperate to see me that he was willing to mortgage himself to do it, I agreed to go. I farmed out the kids, and my dear friend Joanie took my patients for me. Three days later, I was on a plane to Mexico. I had no idea what to expect, though I had a pretty good notion that romantic strolls and happy sexual romps were not in the offing – his melancholy was such that holding hands had become a big leap. Go figure – with all the guys out there begging me to have sex with them, sometimes even with their wives, too, I had to fall for the one guy who couldn't fin his libido with a flashlight, map and GPS tracker.

38
Paradise to Hell (and Back)

LIKE ME, MY friends found it a big mystery. The few casual sexual partnerships I had, dwindled to nothing in large part because I kept feeling drawn back to Bruce. When I told my friends that I was going to see Bruce in Mexico because I didn't want to abandon a friend in need, I knew I was also trying to convince myself of this. In truth, I believed (or wanted to believe) that Bruce was in love with me. I told myself he was just going through a rough patch and if I were there for him, he'd be there for me one day too. And at first, it looked like I'd made the right decision.

He picked me up at the airport and drove me to the apartment complex where he was staying. It reminded me of something in a post card – small apartments clustered around a pool, palm trees, buff young men and women lying in the sun drinking beers and tequila sunrises. I instantly felt relaxed. That night we had a great time, which included dinner, drinks, and a moonlit walk on the beach. He even laughed a few times, which, sad to say, seemed like a big deal. The weather was beautiful and the beach was right outside our back door. What could be better? I spent several hours just sitting on the balcony, watching and listening to the dark waves rolling in. I felt all of my tension and pain seep out of me, until I felt a sense of tranquility like the feeling you have between a giant orgasm and the moment you fall asleep. Everything seemed right with my world, with Bruce's world, with our world.

That feeling lasted about twelve hours.

Beginning the next morning and continuing throughout the second day, Bruce's behavior underwent a not-so-subtle change. He seemed to become cold and removed, as if I were somehow intruding on his space just by being there. I put on my bathing suit and headed to the beach hoping against hope that if I left him alone for a little while, yesterday's Bruce would return. By the time I got to the beach, I'd convinced myself that seeing me in a bathing suit had turned him off. So I somehow managed to convert his emotional problems into a problem with my thighs.

How do we women manage to do that? All it takes is one guy looking at us the wrong way to trigger hours or days of introspection and contemplation about all the things we don't like about ourselves. Is it possible Bruce would not be acting this way if I were taller/thinner/younger/prettier/smarter/richer, etc.? After just an hour on the beach – the same beach that yesterday had left me feeling so peaceful and euphoric – I was now feeling fat, old and unattractive. What a way to spend a Mexican vacation. Shit.

I was supposed to stay for four days but on the third day I decided to cut things short when I overheard Bruce on a phone call with his ex-wife. He told her he missed her, with all the same warmth he'd used to get me down there, and which had ironically disappeared once I'd actually arrived. I all but ran out of the house and headed to the beach to get my thoughts together. When I returned, I let him have it. It was a barrage that was (obviously) long overdue, even if it was not my first with him. I told him I was sick of his bullshit and that as far as I was concerned he'd lied to me about everything. I'd tried to take care of him but I was now convinced it was all part of an act designed to keep me dangling on the hook. He wanted me to be there for him when he needed me so he did what he needed to do to lure me in, and when he got tired of me or just plain bored, he withdrew and called his ex-wife. For all I knew, he was doing the same thing to her, becoming suddenly cold and indifferent to her when he was with me, and then reversing course whenever it seemed she'd had it with him and was jumping ship.

As I stood there yelling at him, he just sat there looking at me. He didn't argue with me, deny anything, or admit anything. It was as if I were practicing a speech and had asked him to sit there as a pretend audience. You never would have known that he was involved in the conversation. His refusal to engage – even to defend himself – in the face of my tirade told me all I needed to know. I told him to go screw himself and headed to the bedroom to pack my bags.

I called United Airlines and changed my return to that afternoon. I said nothing to Bruce other than that I needed a ride to the airport. I flatly told him that he was going to take me whether he wanted to or not. I didn't expect him to argue, and he didn't. He drove me there in silence. My plane didn't leave for another five hours but I didn't care; I'd rather have spent that time standing on the side of the road than have to spend another minute with Bruce.

As I sat in the airport I felt dazed, as if I'd just been in a car accident and hadn't quite processed what had happened. Once I was on the plane, my head finally started to clear. I was heartbroken and relieved at the same time. And I felt even more relieved when I got off the plane in Houston to make a connection, and discovered three tearful messages from him waiting on my cell phone. It was almost comical. When I was in the living room with him he wouldn't engage emotionally or at any other level, but now that I was gone he was crying and telling me he couldn't live without me. A combination of anger and amusement washed over me. But it felt different, too. The heartbreak was still there, but his act wasn't working on me anymore. Back on the plane, I looked up at the oxygen mask. I imagined myself putting it on and breathing deeply. Let Bruce get his own oxygen, I was finally going to take care of myself.

39

Joy in the Dental Chair

MY FIRST DAY back in the dental office, everyone wanted to know about my romantic getaway. They assumed that the ruddy glow in my cheeks had come from warm sunshine and great sex, not from the crying I'd been doing in between my moments of relief that it was over. As I'd driven to work that morning I'd wondered what, if anything, I would feel comfortable sharing. And as I walked into the office I still didn't know. So I engaged in misdirection, or more accurately, redirection. I responded with a "Don't ask," accompanied by a facial expression that said, "Don't ask." My co-workers knew me well enough to refrain from further questions. In the meantime, I dove into my work, hoping that my patients would help me feel better. And as usual, they didn't disappoint me.

My first patient was an openly gay man who knew all about my sex toy business. Before he could ask about my sex or love life, I asked about his. He promptly told me about his trip to the emergency room the previous week. His friend had gotten a Santa Claus candle stuck in his ass. The thought of having to explain that to the ER intake nurse was so horrifying that I burst out laughing. I started singing "Santa Claus is coming to town." Soon we were both in stitches. And just like that I was back in the groove. Anytime I thought of Bruce or my Mexican fiasco, I imagined this guy in the emergency room, explaining to the nurse how he'd gotten a Santa Claus candle stuck in his ass. That worked so well that I continued to use that image almost any time I felt stressed or anxious.

Later that week one of my most difficult patients was scheduled to come in. Phil was a forty-eight-year-old male who also happened to be autistic. I had been seeing him every three months for eight years. He never spoke a word to me or to anyone in the office. All of his communications were with his thumbs – up for yes, down for no. He lived in a group home, and was participating in a program to maintain his oral health. His visits to me were part of that program, and after each appointment I would follow up with his group home leader to report on his progress.

On this occasion Phil came in for his appointment and I went about our normal banter. "How is your job?" Thumbs up. "How are you feeling?" Thumbs up. "Is your mouth ok?" Thumbs up. But as I finished clipping the bib around his neck and asked him to open his mouth he started to become agitated and refused to open. With a mouth mirror and explorer in hand, I again asked him to "Please open," and finally he did. His mouth was a complete mess. It looked like he hadn't brushed or flossed even once since I'd last seen him. I tried to hide my dismay, and said with only (at least I thought) mild concern, "Hmmm, your mouth is not looking so good today, are you OK?" Phil responded by jerking up in the chair so fast he almost knocked me over. He tore the bib off and shouted, "SHUT UP BEFORE I BITE YOUR TITS OFF!"

These were the first words he'd spoken in the eight years I'd been seeing him. And his first words were that he was going to bite my tits off? I didn't think that was very funny but apparently the rest of the office disagreed. My co-workers, and even some of their patients, all burst into laughter.

It was easy for them to laugh – it wasn't their tits at risk. So I scurried down the hall to get my boss. "Did you hear that? I didn't even know he could talk. I am NOT going back in there!" My boss looked at me and said "Heidi, he isn't that different from some of your dates." More laughter, as the three hygienists standing outside eavesdropping continued to find the situation funnier than I did. But I had to admit my boss had a point; Phil's outburst was no more offensive than what I'd gotten from some of my first dates. So I did what any other well-trained professional would do. I plastered a smile on my face, put on fresh gloves, and told Phil to lie back down and open his mouth. To my great surprise, he gave me a thumbs-up and laid himself back down on the chair. I replaced his bib and proceeded to give him an industrial-strength cleaning without further incident. And Phil returned to answering my questions with his thumbs; apparently the threat against my tits was the only statement he was ever going to make.

Meanwhile, thoughts of Bruce receded into the background. Anal Santa Claus candles and patients biting my tits off had been a pleasant diversion from his emotional dramatics. If I couldn't find paradise in a romantic relationship, maybe I could find at least some peace of mind in my patients' mouths.

40
Boozer Picks Us

MY EXPERIENCES WITH the many men I kept meeting, dating, and dumping (or getting dumped by) led me to believe that the challenges I was facing were not setting me back, but rather were helping me to grow. Yet I sensed that the last part of my growth process was going to be the toughest. The last part was about forgiveness, which had never been my strong suit. I never seemed to get forgiveness right; either I was too willing to forgive (e.g., Bruce), or I was completely unwilling to forgive at all (e.g., my ex-husband). My anger with my ex-husband was so great that it threatened to consume me. This was completely counterproductive, as it had no impact whatsoever on my ex's behavior. I needed to let go of the anger, no matter how much disappointment or frustration I felt.

Bruce was another issue. I didn't want to let go of the part of me that loved him, or the fantasy that our relationship could be different. So, conveniently forgetting how Bruce had acted in Mexico, I decided I wasn't ready to let him out of my life for good, and told myself that if I just did a better job of protecting myself from unrealistic expectations, I'd be okay. I'd have to focus on dealing with my ex-husband, and meanwhile try to figure out a way for Bruce and me to be friends and nothing more. But, one thing at a time.

My children continued to adjust to life post-divorce. The one thing my son loved the most was playing hockey. It was his one escape. Then, devastatingly, he was asked to leave the team. I immediately tried to get to the bottom of this bombshell and was told it was because my ex hadn't paid the team fees, for which he had agreed to be responsible. Even worse, my ex had gotten into a fight with the coach. This was truly a heartbreaking revelation for my son and me.

Meanwhile, my son had very few friends at school, and now no hockey team. I knew I had to pursue different options and began looking into them. We attended visiting days at many local private and public schools that had hockey programs. Our current school district didn't offer a hockey program so he'd have to attend a new school the following year if he wanted to continue to play hockey. I knew that him not playing hockey was simply not an option, so we decided that one way or the other he'd have to attend a new school.

My son was approaching thirteen, so a Bar Mitzvah was also on the horizon. We were no longer members of a temple due to the lack of funds, but a Bar Mitzvah was important to us. I had to find a congregation that would be willing to help us, and even then, I wasn't sure how he'd respond to the pressure of Hebrew school.

I also knew that Gabby's death still bothered both of my children. So it caught my attention when a patient of mine in casual conversation mentioned some Huskie/Shepherd puppies she had just gotten in at her shelter. The last thing I needed was the time, aggravation and expense a puppy would bring. And yet there I was, telling my patient I was interested in adopting one of the dogs.

The following Sunday morning I told the kids to get into the car and not to ask any questions, we were taking a ride. Trying to surprise my inquisitive kids did not go over well. They pressed me the entire drive, with increasing annoyance and frustration, for details of our destination. But I kept the secret. And when we finally drove down a winding country road and pulled into the animal shelter they were speechless. I said, "It's time! I'm so proud of both of you, I know you can help take care of a puppy." The kids were ecstatic.

While arriving early was not commonplace for us, it turns out we had to wait ten minutes for the place to open. We asked for my friend and she came out and told me that the last Huskie/Shepherd puppy had left last night. We were beyond disappointed, but didn't give up and started looking at the other dogs. The kids were determined to leave with a dog, yet none of them seemed right. The shelter was filling up with other people. We watched some people walk out with kittens, but we just were not cat people. Things were looking grim. As we were preparing for a long, sad drive home, a man walked in with a big ball of hair wiggling in his arms.

He said, "I have to return this dog, my wife won't let us keep him."

It was one of the Huskie/Shepherd puppies, and every person there wanted him. The volunteer looked at us and said that since we were there first, we had right of first refusal. It took all of about three seconds for us to scream yes, we want him. We felt he was meant to be ours. We hadn't even gotten home before we'd fallen completely in love with him. Bruce, who I had started talking to again as "just friends" (or so I told him, and myself), said he loved dogs, somehow found out. He kept calling for updates, and said he loved dogs so much that he offered to pay for all of the puppy items and adoption fees we needed. He said he would come over with his girls. Bruce, for once true to his word, arrived with a cage, bowls, a leash, toys and everything else we could possibly need. He also helped sign the dog up for puppy school.

Together we played with our new puppy while we tossed around names. We settled on Boozer, after Carlos Boozer, a Cleveland Cavalier who was popular at the time. All of a sudden it felt like I had a family, which was, of course, what I'd wanted more than anything. I watched my kids playing with Bruce's kids. They all got along great. I imagined that everything was perfect, including the spread of ages among the kids. We could become a blended family with Boozer as the linchpin. I told myself we could all live happily ever after, even though there was a voice in my head telling me I was out of my mind.

But I hung onto the fantasy anyway. I told myself it was all about forgiveness. I told myself I was evolving and learning to forgive people for their misdeeds. What I didn't understand at the time was that this wasn't about forgiveness at all. It was about me trying to convince myself that Bruce was or could become someone he didn't seem to want to be. Eventually, that all became clear. In the meantime, Bruce kept coming and going like my bowel problems – reappearing at times of stress, just when I was least able to fight back.

The puppy training was exhausting, but Boozer was a great dog. The kids were keeping their promises to help take care of him. And like clockwork, Bruce was again breaking his. He didn't call when he said he would, became mysteriously unavailable, and seemed to have more interest in spending time with Boozer than with me. My friend Stacy couldn't take it anymore. One day, she announced a "Bruce-intervention." She told me that she refused to sit back and watch while I tortured myself, time and time again. In an effort to distract me, she introduced me to her old neighbor, Jim, and pestered me until I agreed to go out with him. He was just going through his divorce, which made me leery, but Stacy insisted.

Jim and I hit it off immediately. He was cute, fun, and made me feel sexy and desirable. We both had some issues to overcome, and a serious relationship seemed very far off, if it was even possible. But why worry about all of that when at the moment we were having a lot of fun. Jim was just what I needed. Yet the closer Jim and I got, the crazier Bruce acted.

Bruce reverted to calling me two or three times a day. He continuously told me how much he loved me and needed me and assured me that he was working on his issues. He would say how good we would be for each other's children and how comfortable we were together. We could be ourselves and talk about everything. After a few months of this I again began to think we had something. At most, of course, it was a friendship, but I convinced myself it was something more than that. And again, I fell for it. Jim's divorce was still going on, so Bruce, as inconsistent as he was, felt more available. I gave up Jim and went back to Bruce. Stacy (along with everyone else I knew) was ready to kill me, and looking back on it, maybe they should have. What an idiot I was to let him play with me the way he did!

The worst part was that everyone could see it but me. Even Sam could see it. I'd maintained a friendship with him, and we continued to communicate regularly. Sam finally got so frustrated with me and my complaints about Bruce that he delivered an ultimatum. He was not going to speak to me so long as I maintained contact with Bruce. He said it was so painfully obvious to him, more than 300 miles away, that Bruce was terrible for me, that it was causing *him* pain.

So why couldn't or wouldn't I see it? And what *do* you do, when everyone in your world tells you that you're making a fool out of yourself with some guy, and deep down you know everyone is right, yet you just keep on doing what you're doing anyway? In my case, Bruce finally gave me the push I needed. I invited him to go to a black tie fundraiser I'd been invited to. He told me he couldn't go, that he "just wasn't ready to commit." Strange, but after all the weird crap he'd pulled on me, that was the straw that broke the camel's back. I told him to take his commitment-phobia and to screw himself with it. And I happily called Sam to tell him he could start talking to me again.

41
Crazy Class

LATER THAT SAME day, I got a return phone call from a new divorce lawyer I'd been referred to by one of my patients. She specialized in custody and other family law issues so I decided to hire her. Excited about this new direction, I decided to keep the momentum going. As soon as I'd hung up with the lawyer I called the group program to which the social worker had referred me. I learned it was an outpatient program which would teach me skills to think rationally, and to not react so emotionally. I knew this was the thing for me. Plus, my insurance would cover it 100%, so I had no excuses.

The program involved three classes a week for six weeks. Each class consisted of three hours of group work. My parents, kids and friends all expressed skepticism about my new endeavor. It was easier for them, as it had been for me, to point fingers at everyone and everything other than me. But I felt ready to start taking responsibility for my own actions, so I went.

Most days there were around eight people in the class, with the composition changing from class to class. The class was designed with rolling enrollment, which made for an interesting dynamic, as some of my fellow classmates were, like me, just getting started, while others were almost done. In my group that first night there was also an interesting mix of reasons why people were there. A few had eating disorders and a few had depression. There was a cutter, and a hoarder. I immediately thought of Bruce, and how well he would fit in with this group. I had to force the thought of him out of my head — this journey, which I began to refer to fondly as "crazy class," was for me, not for him or anyone else in my life.

The first day of "crazy class" you had to get up and tell the group why you were there, much like AA. I said, "I'm a strong person, I'm high energy, people usually gravitate towards me. It used to be that when I'd walk into a room I'd light it up. But I feel like my light's been put out. I know it's there but I can't get it to go back on. I also used to be a fun-loving and happy person. Now I feel angry and stressed most of the time. I want to find my light again." I felt myself starting to cry. "I feel like I just can't handle any more." My classmates and the facilitator nodded their heads sympathetically and thanked me. This had felt like a huge admission for me to make, yet they all acted like this was totally normal, which to them it probably was. And even that was helpful to me, to realize that what I was going through wasn't quite as unique as I'd assumed it to be.

And so began Crazy Class. Most of my first class was centered on staying in the moment. We discussed remembering to not get caught up in what may or may not happen but to, instead, try to focus on the now. This was especially useful for me since I'm a classic over-analyzer, constantly letting my imagination run away with itself, and never really being present in the moment. It was time I learned that I couldn't control things that were out of my control.

My third class, which was also my first weekend session, was a "bring your family or friends" class. The idea was to encourage me to bring in people in my life to learn about the program and to share in the group lessons. I was a little hesitant because I'd worked so hard to take personal ownership of the issues I was confronting. But I also knew it was silly to try to do this alone, and to pass up an opportunity to win allies on my quest. Still, my mom refused, after which my other family members followed. So I decided to compromise. I invited one of my closest friends, Maggie, and she accepted.

When class began that Saturday, it didn't take long for Maggie to understand why I called it "crazy class." When we were asked to tell our stories, the first person to speak was a large younger man who was rocking anxiously back and forth in his chair and punching himself in his head. He was sitting next to an elderly couple, who turned out to be his parents. His dad had bruises all over his body. The younger man told the group he was very proud of himself. The previous Sunday he'd gotten very upset because the Cleveland Browns had lost. He said that usually when he got angry he would beat up his dad, but because his dad was going through chemo, he had left him alone. Instead, he'd taken his anger out by driving his car off of the driveway and wrecking the front lawn.

Maggie and I, like the rest of the class, exchanged horrified glances. But the facilitator simply said stoically, "Now let's talk about whether there is anything you could have done to get your anger out, other than driving your car across the front lawn?" The man looked around the room, saw everyone looking at him, and suddenly seemed very nervous. He pulled out a small handheld video game device and showed it to us. He said that his computer games were the only thing that seemed to keep him under control, and that the next time he got angry, he would turn to them instead of driving his car or hitting his dad. "I don't want to go back to the hospital!" he suddenly shouted.

I couldn't bring myself to look Maggie's way. I could only guess what she was thinking. Then the door flew open and an attractive but quite heavy woman burst into the room carrying a few dozen donuts and announced: "I'm Nicole, sorry to be late, but I'm bulimic." As if realizing that her bulimia didn't necessarily explain why she was late, she proceeded to tell us that her stress levels were up because her mother-in-law was visiting from France and interfering with her life. She would sit on the sofa shouting out orders while she knitted. Nicole said, "I've been binging and purging just so that I don't grab the knitting needle and poke her fucking eyes out."

Maggie leaned over to me and whispered, "What the hell are you doing in this class? It's a good thing your mother refused to come. She would have dragged you out by your hair. These people are nuts!" Maggie continued, "And knowing you, by the end of your sessions, you'll be leading the group and having half of these people over for dinner." She knew me well!

In spite of, or maybe because of, the craziness, I continued to attend my "crazy classes," while simultaneously trying to work on my own issues instead of passing judgment on others. As it turned out, I enjoyed every class. The life skills I was picking up – even from listening to these "nuts" – were things I thought everyone should learn. Clichés like "staying in the moment" didn't sound so cliché in the class – they became key pieces of my survival strategy. Likewise, the lesson on "Letting Go" really hit home. Just as I'd divorced my ex-husband, I needed to get a divorce from some of my emotions. And the legalities of my divorce provided the perfect opportunity to practice.

My new lawyer had gotten us a court date for late child support payments, yet the date kept getting postponed. Over and over the date would come, I'd arrange to get the day off of work, and at the last minute my ex's lawyer would get a continuance. Each time I my day off meant no income for that day, which naturally added unwelcome stress.

After this happened for the third time my lawyer finally made a plea to the court and got our hearing rescheduled for one afternoon the following week. She told me that this court date would stand. So I left work at 3:30 P.M., and ten minutes later, as I was driving to the courthouse, my attorney's secretary called to cancel, supposedly because my own attorney had fallen ill. At that moment I understood why the guy in my "crazy class" had felt motivated to drive his car in circles on his front lawn. I was ready to the same to my ex's lawn, and maybe my lawyer's, too.

I was going to need every one of those new life skills I'd learned. I made it home safely, took a deep breath, and took Boozer to the park for a walk. As I was walked through the woods along the little creek that ran through the park, I tried to stay focused on the serenity of the woods, and the more positive pieces of my life – my kids, my strengths and the challenges I'd already successfully overcome. It was a struggle, but I could feel myself starting to calm down.

Out of nowhere, I heard what sounded like a drum echoing through the woods. It was a mesmerizing sound, so I followed it. I came into a clearing by the creek. There was a rock in the middle of the creek.

A ray of sunlight was illuminating it. And on the rock was a lady playing what looked like a Native American drum. The drum itself was as beautiful as the sounds coming out of it. I came up to the bank, close enough to see that there was a woman's face painted on the drum. The face was round, and framed by long, flowing blonde hair. I looked at it disbelievingly – it looked like me! I wondered whether this was actually a dream; the quiet warmth of the woods and the hypnotic drumbeat had combined to make me feel I'd been transported to a different time and place, as if I'd just walked into Brigadoon. Even Boozer, who was usually hyper out in the woods, and typically barked whenever he met someone new, just sat there perfectly still, almost as if a spell had been cast on him.

The woman, while continuing to drum, did not acknowledge my presence. I sat down on a tree stump and after a few minutes I finally decided to interrupt. I asked her if she'd mind if I sat and listened a while. She said, "No," without even looking up at me. I felt uncertain. Did "No" mean "No, I don't mind," or did it mean, "Go away?" I felt put off by what I interpreted as rudeness. So I got up and started to walk away. But I'd taken only a few steps when I heard her call, "Wait, did you see that blue heron that just flew by?"

I hadn't seen it, but it didn't matter. She explained that her sister had just died from cancer and the blue heron had been her sister's favorite bird. She'd wanted to be alone, but felt that the blue heron was a message that we should talk. She turned and looked at me for the first time. She seemed startled, and looked from my face to her drum, then back to my face and back to her drum. Finally she said, "The face on the drum is your face. Same almond shaped eyes, same round face and same long blonde wild curly hair. It really is a sign."

She looked at me closely and said, "You're an angel sent here by my sister," I was shocked. She thinks I'm an angel?

We talked for over an hour about her losses and my situation. We listened to each other, gave each other advice. I felt closer to this woman I'd just met than to anyone I'd known in a long time. It was as if she could sense what I was thinking. She said, "I love the energy we have. I'd like to close our circle with a smudging ceremony." Without waiting for me to ask what a smudging ceremony is, she pulled out some sage, a Native American bowl, and some matches. She burned the sage in the bowl, and then twirled the bowl in a circle around us while reciting incantations in some language I didn't recognize. She thanked me, and I burst into tears without understanding what I was even crying about. We exchanged e-mail addresses and said goodbye.

As Boozer and I headed home, I felt like a new person. All I could think about was how much I had to be thankful for. I knew I was a good person, a great mom, and a wonderful friend. In that moment, I knew I was special. I felt my light coming back on for the first time in a very, very long time.

Later, I made many attempts to find the woman I had met in the park, but they were all unsuccessful. She didn't respond to my e-mails, and though I checked that spot on the creek every time I visited the park, I never saw her there again, either. How ironic. She thought I was an angel sent to her, while I thought she was angel who'd been sent to *me*.

At my "crazy class" I told the group about the lady and the drum. Weeks later at my graduation, several group members told me how much the story had affected them, and that it had given them a new sense of hope. I may not have been leading the class as Maggie had predicted, but I felt as though I'd learned enough to teach a class of my own. Crazy Class had worked!

42

Animal Magnetism

THANKS TO CRAZY Class I was on a roll. I knew it, and I wanted everyone else to know it, too, especially my skeptical family and co-workers. I decided that a great place to start would be to show them (and myself) that I was really over Bruce. It was time to hit the dating world again. Besides, I was almost three-quarters of the way to that 100-date mark.

I returned to the Internet and soon started exchanging messages with a guy who seemed very nice. He lived about sixty miles away, which seemed perfect to me. I could see him once or twice a week when I felt like it, but I wouldn't have to deal with anything than I could presently commit to. It could be like Bruce in reverse, I thought.

For the first few weeks, it actually seemed to be working. We went out on three dates, and he made me laugh and seemed very attentive. I was even beginning to think that this could go somewhere beyond the hook-up phase. Until our fourth date, that is. We were out for dinner and I ordered a blue cheese salad. He looked at me with pure disdain. He then stood up, and proclaimed he hated blue cheese and could never date, let alone kiss, someone "who eats mold." He walked out and left me with the blue cheese and the bill. I'm serious. That really happened. How did these guys get like this, and how did I keep managing to find them? It was a question I would find myself asking many times as I continued my dating quest.

Fortunately, I was very busy again with parties, which left me with little time to reflect on the sorry state of my dating life. A couple of weeks after Crazy Class had ended, I had four parties scheduled in a seven-day period. The first of them was being thrown by a sixty-five-year-old woman, who had convinced me to run a party on a Wednesday night for her and seven friends. I was hesitant to pack up my car and run a party for such a small group of older women, but she'd promised it would be worth my while. When I arrived, nine women were there, drinking wine and whooping it up. Before I even got both feet in the door one woman asked, "Do you have lube?" I said yes, and she said, "Great, I'll take a gallon!" The party lasted only one hour but I sold over $900 worth of products, batteries included. I drove home hoping that I'd still be having that much fun with my girlfriends at their age.

The next night I ran a party in an apartment. My sample line at that time had about 150 items in it, and I typically carried five to six large bins worth of inventory with me as well. The apartment was on the fourth floor and I couldn't find a working elevator. After dragging my sample line up the four flights of stairs, I discovered that the apartment was very small to begin with, and woefully overcrowded. The party was going to be in the kitchen/living room/dining room, and the hostess was planning to cram eighteen people into a space that could comfortably fit maybe six. There was barely room for me and my sample line, which meant my inventory would need to stay in the car.

The hostess was a young teacher who had been referred to me by one of my patients. She was very nice and was trying very hard to make the party as fun as possible despite the close quarters. She was also a bit shy, but in a friendly sort of way. She nodded at me and I got up to start the show. As I stood up, I noticed that the hostess' cat had jumped onto the kitchen table and was sniffing at the lotions and licking the vibrators I'd laid out there. The hostess shooed him down, at which point, as if to show his indifference to me, he immediately began to take a crap in his litter box, which happened to be right under the table.

The room was so crowded, and the litter box so close by, that the smell of the cat's poop and urine mixing with the ammonia in the litter quickly became overpowering. I tried to keep talking but instead I started to dry heave and gag. The guests started to notice too, and began making faces. The hostess opened the only window in the room and tried to get some air circulating, but it wasn't working. I finally couldn't take it any more, and said, "Sorry girls, but we're done. I've got a lot of great stuff in my car, if anyone is interested come down to the parking lot to check it out." Amazingly, even though it was drizzling out, I sold more than $400 worth of stuff out of my car. I could only wonder how much more I might have sold if that damn cat hadn't crapped when it did.

The very next night I ran my third party in a row. This one was for another co-worker, Shari. It was going to be my biggest party of the week, with about forty women expected. Shari was hot to get the "Decadent Indulgence" vibrator I'd been telling her about at work. The Decadent Indulgence was not cheap ($125 retail) and Shari was determined to generate enough Passion Dollars to get it for free. She proudly told me that afternoon that she had lots of horny friends and that they were all coming to the party, so I should bring plenty of extra merchandise. Needless to say, I was more than happy to oblige.

The night of the party, Shari's boyfriend decided for some unknown reason to drop his bulldog, Gus, off at her place. Shari warned us all before the party began that Gus "likes to hump." We all laughed and I commented that it might actually be appropriate to have a humping dog at a sex toy party.

We all had appetizers and a few drinks. Then Shari turned the music down and announced we were getting started. I went through the usual routine, and told everyone that I'd pass some samples around and then would explain how the toys worked before heading to a private room to answer questions and help them select their merchandise. This seemed a perfect crowd for my purposes; they were horny and a little bit rowdy, but were generally willing to shut up when I was talking. As I took out my samples I was feeling optimistic about my sales prospects.

This group seemed a bit more advanced than most, so instead of beginning with feathers and lubes, I started with light bondage and then moved to the vibrating cock ring – what better gift to give your man? I was really hitting my stride when I felt something on my leg. It was Gus the Bulldog. He'd wrapped himself around my leg and started to hump. I tried shaking my leg but he had a death grip on it and wouldn't let go for anything. He was going at it a mile a minute. I yelled to Shari for help, and she hurried over and tried, unsuccessfully, to pull him off. Forty women watched and burst out with laughter as Gus finally let go, leaving a great big shot of doggy cum running down my pants.

Some comedian in the crowd yelled out, "Hey Heidi, you really do have animal magnetism!" More laughter. I laughed with them as I wiped off the cum, and kept laughing all the way to the bank, selling nearly $2000 worth of products. Shari was also happy because she got her Decadent Indulgence. As I drove home in my nearly empty car, it occurred to me that the only romance I'd gotten lately was with my friend's boyfriend's bulldog. Could I count that as date number seventy-eight? Granted, the bulldog had his good points – he wasn't emotionally needy and was unlikely to ever walk out on me in the middle of a date. But I decided that I should be able to do better than a bulldog, even one as horny as Gus.

43

Stranger Danger

THROUGH THICK AND thin I stuck to my fantasy that by the time I'd hit the 100-date mark, I'd have met Mr. Right. If I wanted to, I could have had those 100 dates in just a month or two. My Internet dating profiles (yes, plural) were getting 500 hits a week. It didn't matter which site I tried – JDate, Match.com, or eHarmony, there seemed to be a limitless supply of men out there, all of whom claimed they wanted nothing more in life than to meet me.

Unfortunately, most of the men I heard from seemed pretty strange. And that's putting it mildly. Here are some examples, like Jerry28:

> *"Heidi, I thought your profile was very nice and you are very cute. I winked at you and when I didn't hear back it reminded me of high school and how the pretty girls would turn their head or be what we called stuck up. You're fine and very pretty, but I really hope you're not one of those stuck up girls."*

"Winking," by the way, is a device offered on some of the dating sites to let someone know you're interested without having to spend a lot of time writing a message. Depending on your point of view it's a great idea, or it's a lazy way for a guy to send feelers out to dozens of women at a time just to see whether any of them will write to him.

It really irritated me that a guy I'd never met would question whether I was "stuck up" just because I hadn't responded to his stupid wink. So against my better judgment I wrote back and told him I hadn't responded because I'd been ill the past three days. He replied and begged for forgiveness. I wrote and told him I accepted his apology but that he wouldn't be hearing from me again; I don't need a guy who already has to apologize for his behavior before we've even met. Perhaps his willingness to say "I'm sorry" was a good quality, but I figured that a guy should be able to avoid doing anything that requires an apology at least until we've had our first date.

Then there was HiJynx123:

> "I can't believe my luck!!! I'm going out on a limb, because I think you may be way out of my league. I have to tell you that your smile is what caught my attention!!! VERY NICE!!! I assume you read my profile, please don't think that I have a bad attitude towards women. I was trying to come across as funny, and the more I look at it, it makes me sound like a whiner. Anyway I'm far from that. It's just that I don't want any high maintenance gold diggers who are out to use men for their money, I've been burned by that too many times before."

That was his pick-up line? "You have a great smile, I just hope you're not one of those gold-digger bitches who've screwed me in the past?" How romantic! Even I didn't write back to this one. Although, I could have thanked him for being honest and making it so easy for me. Some men are challenging because they do such a good job disguising their dysfunction or even convincing you that their dysfunction is actually *your* dysfunction.

Those guys are truly dangerous. But guys like Jerry28 and HiJynx123, who can't help displaying their insecurity and/or their anger toward women even when they're trying to woo them, are much easier to stay away from. And they become easier and easier to avoid, the more of them you meet. So take it from me, if on or before the first date, a man tells you that you're "out of his league," believe him and move on. And if he asks you to reassure him that you're not a bitch like all the other women he's ever known, tell him you are one, that you're not right for each other, and offer to split the check. Better yet, do it on the computer before you've invested an hour and a glass of wine. Running is hard, clicking is much easier!

Around that time, I had a string of one-night meet-and-greets. None of them went well. I went into each one genuinely convinced that this one would be different from all the other oddballs I was meeting, but each time I'd walk out revolted, frustrated, or just plain disappointed that these guys were all so strange.

Looking back on it, I wish I'd had a therapist read my profile, to see why dysfunctional men seemed so attracted to me. Then again, maybe the problem was that my profile did such a good job of describing me that men could see how dysfunctional *I* was.

Then I met Frank. He was a great-looking Italian guy. I had grown up in a largely Italian neighborhood and had sometimes felt I'd been a pure-bred Italian in another lifetime. Frank was a friend of a friend. We met by chance as I was dropping off some merchandise to my friend's house, so Frank had learned about Heidi's Passion even before we were introduced. I found it a bit of a relief because it saved me some of the uncomfortable explanations I had had to fumble around with so often in times past. He flirted with me and made a few jokes about the bags' contents, but said he gave me credit for doing what I had to do for my kids. He was a single dad as well, and raising his two on his own. His wife had passed away from breast cancer the year before. He seemed genuine, and I felt an immediate connection with him. He was brand new to the dating scene, having just decided to start going out again and he seemed unsure of himself. To me, that was a total turn-on, just as it had been with Sam.

At the end of our third date, he finally kissed me. After a few minutes it became very passionate. I put the brakes on before we got carried away. I got out of his car and all but ran into my house, after telling him, a bit more breathlessly than I would have liked, that I would love to see him again. I was scared to death of him. He was hot, fun and an all-around great guy, with no obvious dysfunctions or offensive quirks. This left me excited and uncomfortable, in equal measure. When he called me later that night to say goodnight I let it go to voice mail. I listened as he went on and on about how much he enjoyed being with me, and how he couldn't wait to see me again. I should have been thrilled. So why was I freaking out?

As usual, I analyzed the situation endlessly. I did it in my head, on the phone with my friends, and with my patients. I noted that we'd met each other just six weeks earlier, and six weeks isn't as long as it might seem for a relationship. The fact that Frank hadn't dated much also frightened me. I worried about getting hurt. I worried about hurting him. And of course I felt it necessary to share all that with him on the phone before our next date. Amazingly he seemed to take my over-analysis in stride. We planned our fourth date.

When our date finally came we went out to a romantic restaurant. Good food, good wine. Everything was fantastic, until dessert when he said, "Heidi, we've been on four dates, I really like you, you're sexy and fun. I've spent a lot of money on you and waited patiently, so are we going to fuck tonight?"

The old Heidi would have wanted to talk about it. She would have asked questions, tried to understand why he felt that way, maybe even offered some sort of compromise like oral sex now and fucking on the fifth date, just to placate him.

But this was the New Heidi. And the New Heidi looked at him calmly. She took the napkin off of her lap and placed it on the table. She stood up, placed a couple of twenties on the table, and in her most ladylike manner, as she turned to leave the restaurant, said "Go fuck *yourself*, Frank." That felt *good*. I liked the New Heidi!

44
The Good Pain in my Neck

I NEEDED A break. The madness of my life was taking its toll on my health. My colitis was flaring up again – maybe all the stress that I'd tried to move out of my head had gotten lodged down there. I was also having neck troubles. The work of a dental hygienist is not forgiving to the hands or neck. I'd already had carpal tunnel surgery in both hands and now I was in physical therapy three times a week for my neck. The best part was the great massages from the good-looking thirty-something massage therapist who was taking care of me. To my friends I started referring to him as "Mr. Hot."

A few weeks into treatment, I walked in for therapy and the usual receptionist was out. The person taking her place said I looked familiar but we at first we couldn't place each other. Halfway through my appointment she came up to me with a Heidi's Passion catalogue in hand and said, "This is you! I was at a party you did a while ago." As we both laughed I thought Mr. Hot was going to faint. His smile (and at least in my own imagination, maybe something else) got even bigger when the receptionist, who was young and pretty, asked if she could book a party. It was always so amazing to me how many people wanted to have these parties. Don't get me wrong, I was thrilled, and felt very lucky that the opportunities kept appearing with relatively little effort on my part. Thank goodness for horny people! I finished my session with Mr. Hot and we set up her party.

The next time I went back for a treatment, I was informed I was going to be seen by one of the female therapists instead of Mr. Hot. I was disappointed, but shortly thereafter Mr. Hot came in with a female therapist, gave me a smile and a wink, and said, "Lisa will be taking over your case." Before I could say anything, Lisa's fingers dug into a pressure point and the pain shut me up. Lisa turned out to be pretty good, so I decided not to complain about the transfer. But still I wondered why.

As I was leaving the office Mr. Hot approached me and asked if I wanted to know why he couldn't see me anymore. I nodded, and he said, "It's because I can't date a patient." My mind had already wandered off to some of the fantasies I'd had as his hands worked me over in past visits, so I failed to immediately grasp the implications of what he'd said. But I managed to figure it out and asked whether that meant he was asking me out. He said yes, and I said yes. And so I left my appointment that day with no more neck pain, a party already scheduled with the new receptionist, and a date with Mr. Hot. Not bad for a Saturday morning!

As it so often happens, Mr. Hot turned out to be more fun to look at and fantasize about than he was to date. But his receptionist was another story – she was a fun client. She lived in an upscale neighborhood, and her party was attended by thirty very attractive, well-dressed women from their early thirties to late forties. (Mr. Hot would have had a field day). Most were married and wanted to talk about learning new ways to keep their marriages healthy, until one of the younger ones spoke up and said, "Forget our husbands. How about our boyfriends?" I was shocked (and a little confused about how to feel) to learn that at least half of the married women had lovers on the side. But the good news for me was that they purchased two of everything – one for their husbands and one for their boyfriends. They seemed less concerned about keeping their infidelity a secret, than about how to tell their husbands' and boyfriends' toys apart. I suggested a little dab of red nail polish on the side of their husbands' toys, pink on their boyfriends'. Nobody but them would ever notice, and they didn't have to worry about it washing off.

Female infidelity was new territory for me. The woman in me wanted to believe that married couples could be monogamous and have great sex, too. But the salesperson in me recognized what a great marketing opportunity an affair presented. So when the conversation turned to bondage – which a surprising number of the partygoers said they were into – I suggested one set of "starter" kits for their husbands, and a slightly more adventurous set of toys for their boyfriends. And it worked – I ended up selling twice as much merchandise as I otherwise would have. The lesson was clear – affairs might be bad for our nation's moral fiber, but they're great for the sex toy business.

45
Church Blessings

I EVENTUALLY LEARNED that the key to successful dating is to not take it too seriously. I treated it as a game, a form of entertainment like a good TV show. I went through the motions of letting people fix me up. My patients continued to pass my number out, and I suspect many were using my side job as a dating tag line, because I occasionally got comments from men asking me whether they could bring a vibrator on our first date, or " I would love you to use me as a demo man."

That second one always got the same response. I'd smile and say, "You'd stand up in front of a group of women and let me shove a dildo up your ass?" I wasn't sure of whom I should be more wary – the guy who said, "Never mind, yecch," or the guy who enthusiastically answered, "Sure!"

The next party was for my patient, Mrs. Robeson, who had asked me to do the party for her ladies' church group. Heidi's Passion had been growing so fast that I'd become unable to cover every party, so we had begun training a few new salesgirls. Mrs. Robeson had told me to expect a full house, so I figured this was a good training opportunity for one of the newbies.

My trainee's first assignment was to help me navigate to the party. She read the GPS directions out loud to me as we drove across town and ended up in front of a beautiful old church. I tried not to let on to my trainee just how weird this suddenly felt. I was about to demonstrate and sell sex toys in a church? Was this evening going to end with me condemned to Hell?

We began carrying boxes and bins into the church basement. The ladies were dressed to the nines and the room was buzzing with conversation and occasional giggles, more like what you'd expect from high school girls than from grown-up women. I managed to get the crowd under control, started the party off with my usual brief introduction, and quickly moved onto the "romance" items. (No bondage or anal plugs in church, I had told myself.) I was trying to remain in character, but each "Amen" and "Hallelujah" that they were yelling out was making it difficult for me not to giggle. Apparently sex really was a religious experience for some of these ladies!

Eventually I moved on finished with the oils and feathers, after which I finally worked up the nerve to start talking about oral sex. But I'd barely mentioned the phrase "oral sex" when a woman who looked to be well over 60 years old stood up and said, "Go slow, I ain't never put that thing in my mouth. Can you show us how to give a blow job"? Never one to back down from a challenge, I called her up and I took out one of our "lollicocks." I started instructing her on what to do. "You wet your lips, stick out your tongue and begin licking and teasing the tip…"

The other women started yelling, "Yes you can!" "Come on sister, you can do it!" "Go Mama!" They were so funny that I finally started relaxing and even getting into it. I told her to open her mouth, cover her teeth, and to start sucking. The next thing I knew she had started dancing around the room yelling and singing, "I could suck a diiiick, I could suck a diiiick!" The others were shouting out choruses of "Hallelujahs!" They were singing and dancing so energetically that I felt I'd been transported into a Baptist revival, except one based on sex instead of God.

I started dancing with them, and blurted out, "This is great, but I'm Jewish so if anyone starts shouting, 'Praise Jesus,' I'm out of here!" They started laughing and stopped dancing long enough for me to regain control of the party. I moved on to the vibrators and by the time we were done the church ladies had bought me out of a ton of inventory.

Back in the car, my trainee looked at me in amazement, and asked, "How did you do that?" I explained that it was simple salesmanship. You need to be a chameleon. Every party has its own personality. Some are mostly educational and some are more fun. The church, of course, had been one of the fun ones. You just need to learn to read the crowd.

In that sense, the parties weren't very different from my dating life. Each date had its own personality, and the key was to be able to read the situation and conduct myself accordingly. As Sam once told me, finding a partner is easy, it's no different than going to a grocery store. Before you go you make a list so you can be sure you don't forget to get the stuff you really need. And when you get to the store, try not to fill your cart with so much crap you don't need that there's no room for what you really do need.

So don't go out dating until you have a pretty good idea of what you want. And don't fill your time with guys who don't have what you're looking for; because if you do, you won't have any room in your cart when Mr. Right finally comes along.

46
Alcohol is Not My Problem

WITH THE PARTY business booming, my health improving, and Mr. Hot in my rear view mirror, I again returned to online dating. The first few guys I met were neither good enough nor bad enough to be interesting. Then Scott came along. After a few chatty email messages we agreed to meet at a bar near my house. To my relief he looked like his photos. We sat down and when I ordered a glass of wine, the first thing he said to the bartender was, "Put that on a separate bill." In principle I'm okay with that – I don't need a man to pay for me all the time, though it did seem a bit odd that he said it to the bartender without asking me. But then I learned why – as if he knew I'd thought his behavior odd, he turned and told me he was a recovering alcoholic. Fair enough, but he then added that he would not, in any way, contribute to my "drinking problem."

I knew I had a lot of problems, but it was news to me that ordering a glass of wine at the beginning of a date was evidence of a "drinking problem." I chatted with him long enough to be polite, which meant I got to hear about his bad kids, bad job, bad marriage, and overall bad life. I wanted to tell him that if I didn't have a drinking problem before, dates with guys like him were going to give me one. Instead I just told him that in addition to all the other "bad" things in his life, he could add a bad first date with me. Needless to say I didn't hear from him again.

The next guy, Owen, was very open and honest. He asked me if we could meet at Starbucks because he did not drink. I agreed, even though I couldn't help but wonder whether some alcohol rehab group had encouraged its members all to go on online and seek me out.

We'd had several conversations before our date and had already gotten some of the preliminaries out of the way on the phone – number and ages of kids, how long we'd been divorced, etc. His kids were coming to visit for the holidays and I offered him some extra movie premier passes that were given to me by a patient. I promised to bring them with me on our first date.

On our first date the conversation quickly turned – at Owen's prompting – to the tricky subject of past dates. Even after all this time I was still waffling about how and when to reveal my party business to men I wanted to date. I'd tried revealing it immediately, and had tried hiding it as long as I could. Neither option seemed ideal. In this case Owen seemed very open so I opted for the immediate reveal option. I'd gotten used to odd reactions, though his still managed to surprise me – he asked if I had any of my toys with me. As if I would normally carry them with me to a first date, especially one on Sunday afternoon at a Starbucks?

But to my surprise, I actually liked his question. So I smiled politely at him and said "I've gone out with about 75 different men, and you're the first to ask me that. You win the grand prize, a trip back to my house where I will let you pick something from the goodie box." Sadly, he took that as a green light to share things I really didn't want to know. I didn't mind, and in fact, felt a bit intrigued by his great interest in kinky sex play. (Maybe that was how he'd gotten his mind off alcohol)? But when he told me he loves it when a big vibrator gets shoved up his ass, I decided I'd heard a little too much information for a first date. So I lied that I had to go pick up my son, and left.

I didn't respond to his phone calls over the next few days. The movie premier was several days later and I decided to use the passes for myself, my friend Gina and her kids. We were in our seats, chatting about the upcoming holidays and waiting for the lights to go down, when I spotted Owen coming in with his kids. Before I could react he spotted me, came up to us, leaned over and gave me a hug as if we were old friends. He introduced his children and sat in our row, with him directly to my right. Gina could barely hold in her laughter. He tried to hold my hand the entire movie. I avoided it by keeping my hands busy eating popcorn. By the end of the movie I wanted to throw up, partly from fending him off, and partly from the giant tub of buttered popcorn I'd finished off single-handedly.

Apparently my cool treatment of him didn't go over well. The next day he sent me an e-mail telling me that I was a nasty person for leading him to think we would have wild sex, and then ignoring him. He said I should be ashamed of my behavior. At least he didn't tell me I was a bitch for forgetting the movie tickets.

After dates with guys like Scott and Owen, all I could ask myself was what I'd asked myself about the blue cheese guy – who are these nuts, and how do they keep finding me? Or, was it me finding them? Or, was I just as much of a wacko as they were? I couldn't help wondering whether I might be better off packing up a bunch of products and taking my show on the road, becoming the first travelling sex toy saleslady. Make the road my home, forget about settling down, and forget about trying to forge a long-term relationship with a guy who's disappointed if I fail to shove a dildo up his ass by the end of our second date.

47
Hummerman

WINTER IN CLEVELAND sucks, except for the holidays. In my first holiday season post-Bruce, my daughter was in Florida with my parents and the rest of our family. My son and I stayed home due to his heavy hockey schedule. Having grown up in a predominately Catholic neighborhood, I'd often considered myself the "wandering Jew" at Christmas time, so I was thrilled to once again be spending the holiday with my friend Gina and her family. The weather cooperated, giving Gina and her family the white Christmas they'd asked for. But driving home after the party, I discovered that "white" also means "slippery." I somehow lost control of my PT Cruiser at a stop sign and managed to skid off of the road into a small ditch. Many cars stopped to see if we were OK. After all, it was Christmas and for a change people felt the urge to be nice.

One of the cars to stop was an enormous Hummer with a very good-looking male driver who looked to be in his mid-to-late thirties. He asked if we needed help, and I said yes. In my mind that meant, "Call a tow truck for us." But in my son's mind it apparently meant, "Drive us home, marry my mom and become my new dad." Because when the guy we soon came to call "Hummerman" said he needed to go home to get a rope so he could pull us out, and asked did we want to go with him, my son yelled, "Yes, we'd LOVE to go in your car!" I looked at him sternly and said, "How many times do I have to tell you not to get into a car with a stranger?" He said, "Mom, it's not a car - it's a Hummer! I've never been in one!" Ignoring my son's pleas, I accepted the Hummerman's offer for help, but informed him we would stay with the car. While we sat there, I looked at my son and hoped that if a kidnapper ever approached him, he wouldn't be driving a Hummer.

Just ten minutes later the Hummerman returned. With him was a boy about my son's age, and another guy he introduced as his next-door-neighbor. The Hummerman introduced himself as Gary and asked where I lived. When I identified my neighborhood (I was still leery of giving him my actual address), he said, "Hey, my divorce attorney's office is right near you." My son, who was dumb enough to get in a Hummer with a stranger but smart enough to recognize a pick-up line, said, "Mom, he's trying to pick you up." The Hummerman laughed and said, "He's right, here's my card. I'd love to see you again." He and his "crew" winched my car out of the ditch and I was on my way home. I decided to send him an e-mail thanking him for saving the day. He responded with an invite to his country club for dinner. Being a sucker for good-looking guys who help damsels in distress, I quickly said yes.

The date went very well. He was handsome, charming, smart, successful, and funny. I couldn't wait to go out again. When the Hummerman told me he felt the same way, I had visions of the end of my dating saga. Granted, we'd only had one date. But it just *felt* so right. I imagined us continuing to date, falling in love and getting married. His son and my son would become best buddies, I'd become a regular at his country club, and I'd get to borrow his Hummer when I needed extra room for kids or groceries. Irrational, maybe, but a girl can dream, right?

For the first few dates, the story stayed true to form. Unfortunately, life didn't want to cooperate. My dental work and party schedules got very busy, as they usually did after the first of the year. My kids and I also got sick, passing the flu back and forth between us for the better part of a month. I wasn't very available and the Hummerman began to express frustration that I was putting my work and kids ahead of him. I understood his frustration but felt it was too early in the relationship for me to drop everything else for him, and told him so.

He told me my problem was that I was lost and did not have proper direction. He offered to help me. I had no clue what he was talking about. Before I could ask, he dropped the bombshell — he told me he was a born-again Christian, that he had a personal relationship with Jesus Christ, and that if we were to continue to date I would need to find Jesus, too. I told him I was sorry, that I respected his beliefs but that this little Jewish girl had no interest in a threesome with Jesus.

That was the last I heard from the Hummerman. So much for my happy ending, and my country-club membership. It looked like another year of being dentally fixated and teaching about oral stimulation was in the offing. From time to time I still thought about the Hummerman. Maybe I should have introduced him to my church ladies? Though I can only imagine what he might have thought if he'd learned I'd been teaching blowjob techniques underneath a statue of Jesus. Something tells me he might not have considered it a "Hallelujah!" moment like my lady friends had.

48
Someone Call the Cops!

BETWEEN HOCKEY SEASON and a busy party schedule I didn't have much time to date. And after my disappointment with the Hummerman, I needed a break anyway. It was becoming increasingly clear that I was going to meet and exceed my one-hundred date plateau without finding The One. That was depressing me – what was the new number? Two hundred? One thousand? Meanwhile, like an animal who could smell weakness, Bruce had reappeared, starting to cajole me into seeing him again. I felt myself wanting to say yes, like an alcoholic who is trying to convince herself that just a sip or two of alcohol won't hurt.

Fortunately, I was sane enough to see what was happening, and knew I had to get Bruce out of my system for good. To distract myself from him I once more turned to my parties. The first one of the year was hosted by a woman who had met me at the receptionist's party, the one where all the women had bought toys not just for their husbands, but their boyfriends, too. I couldn't remember whether this woman had said she was stepping out on her husband, which was probably just as well, as she told me that her party was for her family, which was "very large" and that they would all be there.

None of my trainees were available, so I brought Maggie along to help. I warned her that I had no idea what to expect from a "family" party. A family reunion, perhaps? Weird, even for me. Maggie and I were left nearly speechless when we walked into her gigantic and well-furnished suburban basement. The hostess introduced us to her mother, and her mother's three sisters, as well as all of the various cousins, aunts and uncles, nieces, nephews and some family friends, too. All told there were about fifty people, male and female, ranging from their early twenties to their seventies, some couples, some single. The hostess said the family shares everything with one another. "No secrets here," she said.

One of the male cousins had just returned from Thailand. He saw fit to share with the group that he had learned to enhance women's orgasms by choking them until the moment they start to cum. He then asked whether we sold liquid latex. I was familiar with it. Liquid latex is a specialized material that you paint on. As it dries it gets hard, and eventually when you're done you peel it off. He said he liked to use it to make it harder for his partner to breathe, and that the oxygen deprivation greatly intensifies her orgasms. I tried not to imagine what that might be like; I found it both intriguing and terrifying, though mostly terrifying. I told him I didn't have any with me – not surprisingly it's not such a big seller – but I proudly let him know we did have it on our website.

He seemed satisfied with that answer. So satisfied that he turned to Maggie, and said, with no hint of embarrassment, "I love older women, do you want to try it? I'd love to choke you to orgasm." Maggie turned beet red and was obviously flustered, so I quickly changed the subject by soliciting questions from the rest of the group. One of the nieces shouted across the room, "Hey Aunt Judy, I bet Uncle Terry would love this!" as she pointed to one of the anal plugs on display. I couldn't imagine discussing this kind of stuff with my own family; it was like being on the Jerry Springer show. And as if to confirm that thought, a catfight broke out between two of the female cousins. It began with shouting and soon the two girls were clawing at each other, throwing punches, and shrieking at the tops of their lungs.

Over the noise of their shrieking I heard someone yell out to call the cops. And suddenly I was yelling, too. I was yelling, "NO!!!" I imagined the police arresting me along with everyone else while they sorted it all out. And my kids seeing their mom on the front page of the *Cleveland Plain Dealer*, or the lead story on the 11:00 news – or both. As various relatives worked to break up the catfight, Maggie and I packed our stuff and got the hell out of Dodge.

Maggie announced her retirement on the way home, and I couldn't blame her. But I had five more parties on the calendar in the next six weeks. So for me, it was full speed ahead, family catfights or no.

49
What Do I Tell the Kids?

AS MUCH AS I struggled with what to tell my dates about my parties, I worried more about my kids. Sometimes arrangements I'd made for child care on my party nights would fall through. I'd be getting ready to leave for a party and at the last minute I'd discover I had no choice but to leave them alone. It wasn't that big of an issue though, my daughter was fifteen by now, and old enough to babysit. Still, I felt terribly guilty leaving them alone. I knew we desperately needed the money the parties were bringing in but I still wondered if it was all worth it.

There was also the question of what to tell them about where I was going on all these evenings. I'd been telling them I was going to "business meetings" or "parties" or whatever had come to mind at the time. But I was becoming increasingly worried my ex would tell them about Heidi's Passion just to spite me, or that their friends would hear something from their parents, and I wanted them to hear it from me first.

So one day I sat them down and started to have a conversation with them about Heidi's Passion. In retrospect, I shouldn't have been surprised that they both already knew. In fact my daughter laughed at me, rolled her eyes, and said, "No shit, half of my high school knows, it's not a big deal, but I do have some questions about some of the stuff in that box in your room."

I wondered just how big of a deal this really was for her. I told her we would talk later in private and in the meantime to stay out of that box.

My son asked how I felt about selling "bad" things. I told him they were not bad, nothing is forced on people. When two adults are in a loving committed relationship, romance is a huge part of it. (No matter how "honest" I was, I simply wasn't ready to talk to an eleven-year-old boy about sex toys. So instead I kept focusing on the "romance" angle). I said, "I'm proud that I help people with their romances. The lesson in this is that no matter what you do in life, work hard, and be proud of who and what you are. As long as you have passion, you will be the best at whatever you're doing."

He thought about that for a moment, then looked up at me with his baby blues and said, "Mom, does that mean you're the best sex salesperson?" I smiled said, "Yes!" He said, "Cool!" Then he gave me a fist pump and went back to his video game. After both kids had left the room I gave myself a little fist pump, too. I'd done well! Now, if I could only figure out how I would handle the conversation with my daughter about that box under my bed. Oy!

50
Swinging it

THE OTHER HEIDI and I were making some needed changes to the business. We were lucky enough to have hired an acquaintance of mine away from one of our competitors. (Yes, the success of our business had, inevitably, attracted some competition. But at least at that point there seemed to be plenty of business to go around, and we didn't really feel any effects from the competition). Linda was an experienced businesswoman who understood the toy business and, unlike me, had the time and energy to devote to it on a full-time basis. I told her that I wanted to be "the show," so to speak, by which I meant I'd be perfectly happy being told what to do, where to go, and to collect a pay check, while letting someone else do all the thinking and planning. Linda brought with her many connections and resources that Heidi and I didn't have. She had promised to help take the business "to the next level." In the sex toy arena I had no clue what the "next level" could possibly be. I soon found out.

Linda had connections with several local sex-related clubs. One of them was simply called "Swingers." Its members engaged in partner-swapping. She had cut a sponsorship deal with them in return for which we got a booth at one of their upcoming events. The event was going to be held at a hotel near Toledo. And she convinced me that as the face of Heidi's Passion, I needed to be the one to man (or woman) the booth.

Having worked a booth before, I was comfortable saying yes, so I agreed to attend. About a week before the event, however, when Linda sat me down to explain the "rules" of this exclusive, invite-only event, I began to have some second thoughts. Here were the rules she gave me:

1. No single women were permitted, but for every ten couples one single male could attend.
2. I was not permitted to join in any sexual acts while attending the event. (As if *that* was a problem)!
3. I must not leave the booth unattended.
4. Discretion was key. If I ran into anyone I knew I was to act as if I didn't know them and never repeat that I saw them at the event.

I stopped listening at that point. It had never occurred to me that I might know someone at a partner-swapping event more than hour's drive away. But what if I did? What if I ran into some of my next-door-neighbors, swapping sex with our high-school principal and his wife? What if they came up to my booth to buy an extra dildo or two? I told Linda she was crazy, that there was no way I could do this. But when she told me there would be more than two hundred participants and I could expect to clear a few thousand dollars for the weekend – yes, a few *thousand* – I decided I could probably do it after all.

As I pulled into the hotel, my car packed to the gills with products, I saw that the hotel's ground-floor windows had been soaped so you couldn't see in. I didn't consider that a good sign. What, exactly, were they expecting to have to hide? I walked into the lobby with one of my larger boxes in my hand and saw the tables with Heidi's Passion signs on them. I set the box down and was starting out to my car when a man approached me. He introduced himself as Kurt, the event contact person. He offered to help me carry in my things. As we were unloading my car he began to review the event ground rules with me. He reiterated what Linda had already told me but added a few kickers. The first was that after midnight, clothing was optional. My stomach tightened a bit as he continued.

There were three types of rooms:

1. A closed door meant, "Invite only."
2. A door propped open meant, "Voyeurs only."
3. A door with an "Open" sign meant, "Free-for-all."

I tried not to think about just what might be going on in the "voyeur" or "free-for-all" rooms. Misinterpreting my distracted gaze, Kurt said, "If you're thinking of playing a bit I could get the security guard to man your booth for a while." I just looked at him, not having any idea what to say. He said, "Think about it," and wandered away. I got started setting up my tables. I had to keep reminding myself not to be judgmental. After all, there were plenty of people who'd pissed me off by judging me for selling sex toys; who was I to judge these people just because they liked to have sex in a group setting?

I had developed a little mantra to get me through some of the kinkier moments in my parties. It was, "To each his own, no judgment." I started repeating that to myself under my breath. I figured I was really going to need it today. I was almost finished setting up when I heard someone call my name. I looked up and standing in front of my table was a couple I knew well; Stuart and Claudia were both dental patients of mine. They seemed excited to see me. Stuart said, "Heidi, wow it's *great* to see you here at this event." The way he emphasized "great," along with his lecherous stare, made me want to throw up, especially as I thought about his halitosis, and all of the periodontal issues I knew he and his wife had. Meanwhile Claudia seemed a little less enthusiastic about running into me. She said, "What are you doing here?" as if that wasn't already obvious.

I told them I was just working, trying to get the point across, without being disrespectful, that I most definitely was not into "playing" with anyone. I'd be working the entire time and would have to pass. They said okay, but as they walked away Stuart winked and said, "Be sure to let us know if you change your mind!" I thought, "Not on your life, buddy," but outwardly I just smiled and gave them a little wave. As they walked away I prayed I wouldn't see anyone else I knew. I didn't think I could handle many more conversations like that one.

My booth was busy nearly nonstop that night, which was great because it gave me little time to think about my surroundings or the cast of characters that I was selling to. It was a very diverse group of people. They ranged in age from early 20s to mid-sixties. Some looked great in the buff and some looked, well let's just say they really should have worn a robe. Not surprisingly, nearly all of them were completely comfortable talking about sex toys, and very knowledgeable. My libido and I went on a roller-coaster ride throughout the night. Some of the couples were pretty hot-looking and talked a *great* game, to the point that I could almost imagine myself joining in. But then they'd be followed by a couple that totally grossed me out.

"To each his own. No judgment. To each his own. No judgment. To each his own. No judgment." I must have said that to myself several hundred times as couples bought dildos, butt plugs, vibrators, blindfolds and handcuffs, riding crops, lubes, and pretty much everything else you could imagine, clearly intending to head straight over to one of the rooms down the hall to use them. Several times I was sorely tempted to wander down one of the halls just to see what the scenes looked like, but the steady stream of people at my table kept me in place.

Well, mostly in place. At one point, when I went to use the ladies' room, I could see down one of the hallways. There was a group of people outside one room, and I heard some sounds that you would normally expect to hear only in the soundtrack of a porno movie. When I exited the ladies' room I couldn't help myself, I had to peek into the large ballroom filled with tangled, sweaty, grunting participants. There were several "love swings" and massage type tables that were occupied. Loud music was playing and the darkness was offset with gentle mood lighting. Several mattresses had been brought in and were on the floor with three or four naked bodies in various positions on them. It was way more than I was able to handle; I scurried back to my table and finished off the evening.

The next day was more of the same. In the end, Cindy's prediction proved accurate; I cleared more than two thousand dollars, which made it the most profitable event I'd ever done. In one fell swoop I'd paid for a nice chunk of my son's bar mitzvah. I drove back patting my newly fattened purse and looking happily at the empty spaces in my car where the boxes of product used to be. Thank you, Swingers!

51
Comfortable in my own skin

I'M NOT SURE why, but after the Swingers weekend, I felt a renewed sense of self. I wanted to have sex. I needed to have sex. But that Swingers' weekend had reminded me how much I also valued intimacy. Since my divorce I'd been getting sex without intimacy, or intimacy without sex. I wanted both, and I wanted them at the same time with the same man. And I was finally at peace with the realization that Bruce was not and could not ever be that man.

Between my dental jobs and Heidi's Passion I had plenty of opportunity to work. Also Linda, true to her word, was helping Heidi's Passion grow by leaps and bounds. We now had four party consultants, which meant I was able to pick and choose the parties that I worked. This gave me a freedom of scheduling I hadn't felt in quite a while. One weekend I decided to exercise that freedom and attend a dental conference in Boston with my boss and a co-worker. I had never been to Boston before and hadn't traveled anywhere since my trip to Vegas. So I was ready to let loose and have some fun. The conference didn't start until Saturday so we spent Friday exploring the city. That night there were several big parties. I got dressed up and felt like a million bucks. This was just what I needed.

At the first party we went to we met an executive named Chris. He worked for a company that sold products to my boss, so Chris' job was to wine and dine my boss, and by extension, my co-worker and me. Chris was young, smart, adorable and single. After the party died down he grabbed a few colleagues and whisked us away to a great restaurant. The night was a blast. He was one of the funniest people I had ever met. I thought my imagination might have been made hyperactive by all the martinis because it felt like he was flirting with me. What would this fun and good-looking twenty-nine-year-old man want with a forty-year old divorcee?

But apparently it wasn't just my imagination. Long after my boss and co-worker had returned to the hotel, Chris and I were in a pub drinking, talking and laughing. I opened up to him and shared some of my career desires and needs. Chris was a bigwig in the industry and very smart. I had come up with a concept for a dental consulting company and pitched the idea and concept to Chris. He thought I was onto something great and encouraged me to continue developing it.

Although nothing ended up happening with Chris other than some more flirting and a very affectionate kiss good night, the weekend had proven fun, educational and great for my self-esteem. I was feeling sexy and attractive again. On the flight back to Cleveland I reminded myself, thinking again of the Swingers party, that a relationship without intimacy is not a relationship. Bruce finally was history. Heidi the sex-toy-saleswoman extraordinaire would never again be in a relationship that didn't include great sex.

My first week back after Boston, I recruited my co-worker and fellow hygienist for my consulting company. We began working and developing a business plan. I also ran into Jim, Stacy's friend, who had been one of the potentially "good" guys I had dumped for Bruce. We started hanging out again as friends. Jim and Sam, who I also continued to talk with regularly, were teaching me the value of having male friends. Whenever I seemed at risk of falling back into a one-sided relationship like I'd had with Bruce, they were there to call me out on it. And maybe it was because Sam had been so right about Bruce, but for whatever reason, the relationship advice I got from my male friends began to mean even more to me than the advice I got from my female friends. They were able to tell me exactly what the latest schmuck in my life was thinking, and why I needed to stay away from him. What a relief!

Meanwhile, Chris and I had kept in touch. We met several times during the next few months. We eventually fell into a romantic relationship. He was a great diversion and source of support. His encouragement helped me both professionally and emotionally. I felt a renewed sense of my own sexuality. Horniness is a good thing, but horniness with a sense of purpose is even better. It helps steer you to look for sex in all the *right* places.

52

An Angel in Disguise

EVEN THOUGH MY kids had taken my admission of being in the sex toy business quite well, I was still having some internal struggles with that part of my life. Things were getting a bit too bizarre for me. The swingers' party, the burglary, all the women I kept meeting who were having affairs, and the ever-increasing publicity associated with the growth of Heidi's Passion were constantly challenging my personal sense of morality. I felt fortunate that Linda and our new consultant had taken over most of the parties, letting me focus more on my dental business. I continued to do a few parties now and then, but by special request only. I took on a party only if I had a special relationship with the hostess, or if we knew the party was really going to be worth my while.

The first party that met those criteria was at a friend's house in Michigan. She was hosting a party for her neighborhood. It was a three-hour drive from Cleveland so I thought about imposing some sort of minimum purchase requirement. But my friend assured me that everyone attending had money and would be ready to spend, so I decided to take her word for it. When I arrived, it seemed that she had steered me right. The attendees were well-dressed and apparently well-heeled Jewish women. They were drinking and having a blast. So I was feeling pretty optimistic when I started the show. But there were two women in the corner who kept saying, "Eew, eew, eew, that's gross!" every time I took out a new product. And their commentary was chilling the room – it seemed nobody wanted to admit they liked something when these two women were loudly expressing their disgust. I pulled out some "Good Head" (a flavored numbing agent that made BJ's easier) along one of my best-selling products, the "Virtual Pussy" (male masturbation aide). I explained that with these two items, a faster, better blowjob could be achieved. I began to demonstrate just how that would work, when one of the women in the corner said, "That's gross. And our husbands don't like blow jobs anyways."

When I realized that nobody in the room was disagreeing with them, I decided I needed to take them on. I stared right at the one who'd just spoken and said, "Lady, *every* guy likes blowjobs. If your husband says he doesn't like them, then you either you don't know how to give one, or he's getting them from someone else, or both." The woman looked at me in shock, and sputtered as if she wanted to say something, but nothing came out. She and her friend kept their mouths shut for the rest of the show, which finally allowed the other women in the room to ask questions and admit they liked what they were seeing.

After the demos were over, I went into a private room to conduct the "sell & consult" portion of the party. The first woman in was the heckler I'd put down. She apologized if she'd come across as rude. She said that in fact it's not that her husband doesn't like blowjobs, it's just that he's more into anal sex, and asked me to show her everything I had for that. The look of shock on my face was clearly visible to her; she just smiled back and purchased several "backdoor" items. You just never know.

I ended up selling more than enough products that night to have made the trip worthwhile. And a month later, when I returned for a non-toy birthday party for my friend, practically every husband at the party came up to me to thank me. That was me, an angel with a suitcase full of devilish tricks. And it's nice to imagine that those tricks have made a lot of people very happy and maybe even saved a marriage or two?

53
Dental or Dildo?

I HAD ALWAYS known that eventually I would have to make a choice between sex toys and dentistry. Trina and I had been spending more and more time on our plans for the dental consulting business. Part of that plan included doing local lectures on dental-related topics. I started doing them and found I really enjoyed talking to a crowd. People really seemed to respond to me and that was just the encouragement I needed. It seemed that the same qualities that made people enjoy my dildo presentations led them to enjoy my dental talks. I was repeatedly asked to visit dental offices to teach the staff how to educate their patients, and I loved doing it.

We started expanding our topics and began incorporating more information on dental implants. The humor of it all was great. People who knew who I was seemed to enjoy hearing "Dildo Heidi" talk about implants. I wasn't sure why, and I did my best to keep them separate, but it turned out that wasn't always possible. One day, Trina and I were giving a lecture to a hundred or so dental hygienists. At the end, we held our usual Q and A session. One woman raised her hand and asked if I was the same Heidi that was at a "party" she'd attended over the weekend. Fortunately she didn't specify the type of party. Trina and I looked at each other and burst out laughing. The woman had her answer, and we returned to implants.

Summer was coming and I was looking forward to some time with my kids and friends. I was using some of the money my four jobs (two hygienist gigs, plus Heidi's Passion and the consulting business) were bringing in to pay for something I'd always wanted, a deck in the back of my house. The men were working on it for so long that it seemed that the deck I'd wanted forever was going also to take forever to build. One afternoon I came home early from work to find the workmen sleeping in the backyard next to a pile of lumber that should have already been part of the deck. I also found that all the beer in my refrigerator was gone, which probably wasn't a coincidence.

I woke the men up and angrily threw them out before calling the contractor who had hired them and giving him an earful. Miraculously, my deck was done in two days. But apparently the workmen had taken more than just my beer; everything in my tool shed was gone, including about $2500 worth of lawn equipment. As I dialed the phone to make a police report I wanted to scream. But instead I found myself laughing. I gave myself a little speech: "I'm a whirlwind, working four jobs to support my kids. I thought I had nothing that anyone could steal from me, yet these guys managed to find something I didn't even realize I had until they'd stolen it. What else do I have to steal? Bring it on, I can handle anything!"

It was the first time in which, even though I'd been victimized, I didn't act or feel like a victim. No more self-indulgent pity parties for Heidi. I would just keep on working and raising my kids and hunting for a relationship – meanwhile everything else is just window dressing. Whatever, bring it on!

54
When You Least Expect It

MY GOOD MOOD, newly-discovered self-confidence and continual horniness didn't change the fact that my dating life remained a roller coaster ride. I was closing in on my one-hundredth post-divorce man (by my latest count I was up to 96). Between my four jobs, I not only had paid for my deck, but I'd also saved enough money to send both of my kids away to summer camp for a month. This was going to be my first extended break from parenting in well over three years, and I told myself it was going to be heaven.

The first week after dropping the kids at camp, I went out with some friends after work one night. A friend of theirs joined us, and he introduced himself to me with, "Hi, I'm David. I'm going to walk you to your car tonight and kiss you goodnight." Feeling a bit playful, I said, "The hell you are," but smiled to let him know I wasn't necessarily saying no. Taking his cue, he laughed and said, "Oh yes, I will." I let him buy me a drink, and then a second.

David wasn't just likeable, he was also impressive. He was an emergency medicine doctor, and very funny. After about ninety minutes of friendly banter, he in fact did walk me to my car, and also kissed me good night. He asked me out to a baseball game the following night and I quickly said yes, partly because I like baseball but mostly because I liked Dr. Dave. He closed with, "We're going to have fun together."

He was right. We went to the baseball game and had a great time. We went out a few more times after that and had fun each night. But his ER schedule was very demanding, and before I knew it my kids were back from camp. On top of all that, he'd accepted a job working as a doctor on a sailboat in Europe for three weeks. (I sure wished those boats hired dental hygienists)! It appeared that he and I weren't relationship material after all. I drove him to the airport and went back home to make the kids' beds and stock the house with groceries. I was sorry to see him go.

By coincidence, just as Dr. Dave left and my kids returned, I was pulled out of my semi-retirement to host two toy parties for people I knew well. One party took place at a friend's restaurant and all of my work friends and neighbors came. They knew I was working my way out of the business, so they all wanted to see me do the "demo" and stock up on products possibly for the last time. We all had a ball and they bought a ton of toys. It was exactly what I'd always hoped the toy party business would be like.

The second party was for a group of middle-aged women who, it turned out, were all (or at least claimed to be) happily married and monogamous. They bought mostly toys designed for couples. It was inspiring and I wondered whether someone was trying to send me a message that it really is possible to be sexually satisfied in a monogamous relationship. I didn't know whether these would be the last two parties I'd ever do, but if so, it was a great way to go out.

Once the kids were back to school and I was back in the swing of things in the dental office, my consulting business continued to grow. I also started dating in earnest again. At one point I was juggling four guys, which might have been fun if I'd really liked any of them. Then Dr. Dave reappeared. He'd been back from his sailboat gig for about a month but his crazy schedule hadn't provided much opportunity for getting together. And surprisingly I found that attractive; his relative unavailability and apparent lack of interest in a committed relationship relieved the pressure I felt from many of these other guys, who after two dates started telling me how I should be raising my kids or complaining that I was putting work or parenting ahead of them. Soon the other four guys were gone and I was dating Dr. Dave exclusively.

Well, not totally exclusively. We hadn't made any commitments to each other, so I felt free – even obligated in a way – to occasionally go on a date with someone else. That Christmas break, I took my kids to Florida to see my parents. While we were there, my ex-husband's aunt fixed me up with her chiropractor. (Yes, I know that sounds weird, but I actually had a much better relationship with my ex's family than I did with him). The chiropractor seemed at first like a great catch, even though he was currently going through a divorce. He was handsome, successful, smart, and fun. Our first date was the usual interview type date, a Q and A session about ourselves. We had an open conversation about dating, and he proceeded to ask me if I dated a lot. I was not sure how to answer the question without laughing out loud, as he was number 100! The first three dates with him were great. I couldn't help but wonder if he really could be The One? He had two young children, a great business and I liked him, so far.

At least until I discovered he'd left out a few things about his life. On our fourth date, he started talking about his son's Bar Mitzvah. I was confused, as he had told me that his children were 5 and 6 years old, not anywhere near 13. He picked up on my expression and said "Oh, did I forget to mention about my three children in New York?" He had been married three times; this was going to be his third divorce. That was the end of that for me.

I felt exhilarated and relieved at having finally reached the 100 man milestone. But I also felt let down that #100 turned out to be such a bust. I decided to give myself permission to stop counting. I'd be content with my non-relationship relationship with Dr. Dave. The lack of drama with him seemed like a breath of fresh air. We may not have had what I'd always considered a "normal" relationship, but at last I had met a guy who didn't seem totally abnormal, either.

The following spring we were still dating, and I was still enjoying myself. He had another sailboat gig coming up that May, this one was to the Greek Islands. One night, he even asked me to join him on the trip. I found this scary. What was I scared of? I was thinking of all of the broken promises men had made to me. I was thinking about taking off time from my job and business. And of course I was wondering who would take care of my kids. Once again my mother came to my rescue, saying, "I'll take them. Go, it's a trip of a lifetime!" My business partners and employers all agreed it was a great idea. So I said yes, I set my calendar, and I made my plans. I was going on a three-week sailboat cruise.

My past experiences told me that something would go wrong. As the weeks went by and the departure date approached, I kept waiting for it to happen. I expected the trip to be unexpectedly cancelled, for Dr. Dave to tell me that he couldn't get away from the ER after all, or that he'd met someone else and changed his mind about taking me. But he didn't. And that May, three years almost to the day after my divorce, I sailed off into the Mediterranean sunset, ready to start what I hoped was a new and wonderful phase of my life, with no ex-husband, Bruce, or sex toys, in sight.

Well, maybe a couple of sex toys. But they were just for me and Dr. Dave. It was about time for me to put those years of training to good use!

The End (for now)

Epilogue

THE SUNNY FEELINGS I had as I set off on my trip with Dr. Dave didn't last long, though through no fault of Dr. Dave. Our departure was delayed by weather, which meant we missed our connecting flight on the east coast. Our rerouting added a full twenty-four hours to our travel time, including an overnight in an airport terminal in Sweden. And to add insult to injury, when we arrived in Malta we waited fruitlessly as our fellow passengers retrieved their luggage. Mine, filled with my favorite clothes, lingerie, and of course my favorite toys, didn't arrive. Dr. Dave and two other women who I learned were to be on our trip were also *sans* suitcases.

It was while chatting with those two women that I learned the nature of the boat trip Dr. Dave was working on – it was a group of Christian evangelists. Great. My divorced Jewish boyfriend and I would be hearing all about Jesus as I carried my suitcases filled with lingerie and sex toys onto the boat.

Well, maybe not, since the airline still couldn't tell us where our suitcases were. They assured us they would arrive before the boat set sail at 5 P.M. the next day. We were skeptical about that promise so we went shopping for essentials, including a couple of new outfits, and basics like cosmetics and underwear.

Oh, and of course it was that time of the month for me at that precise moment, and I'd used up all my feminine hygiene products during our unexpected Swedish layover. Then, while trying on a sundress in a small clothing store, of course the price tag hit me in the eye and gave me a corneal abrasion, causing me eye pain like a motherfucker, as if a knife were stabbing me in my eyeball. My eye kept watering so badly that I could barely see out of it, while every blink caused me ridiculous pain.

So that's how my romantic trip-of-a-lifetime started, with the first night spent sleeping in a Swedish airport terminal, the second night in bed with an ice pack on my eye and horrible menstrual cramps. Dr. Dave told me to stick it out, and that once we got on the ship, the clinic he'd be working in would certainly have eye drops to help me. Meanwhile, we took a tour around the city of Valletta, which I'm sure would have been beautiful had I been able to see it.

The next day we boarded the boat and the first thing we saw was a row of suitcases. Everyone's had arrived except for mine, of course. My trip of a lifetime had turned into the trip from Hell. At least, that's how it started. But as the day wore on, things started looking up. Dr. Dave gave me eye drops and my eye quickly healed. It turned out that the evangelists were fabulously interesting and fun companions. When purchasing my "essentials" the previous day I'd forgotten to buy hair products, so I spent most of the next 20 days looking like a Chia pet. The romance between me and Dr. Dave never really kindled, but I was fine with that. We had a great time together, and I felt warm and cared for and it felt great, even if the romance was lacking and in the end he felt more like a brother than my future husband.

So my Mediterranean cruise turned out to be a replay of my post-divorce life – a horrible, emotion-ridden, tearful beginning, followed by resignation and ultimately acceptance, satisfaction and friendship. And just like in my "real" life, all that was missing was a man. I optimistically believed there would be plenty of that yet to come, even if the who, how and where remained a mystery. But without mystery, what is the point of getting out of bed in the morning?

Stay tuned for Open Wider in 2016.

Made in the USA
San Bernardino, CA
28 November 2015